IMF And The ASIAN Financial Crisis

World Scientific Asian Economic Profiles

IMF And the ASIAN Financial Crisis

Consulting Editor
Peter G. Zhang

World Scientific
Singapore • New Jersey • London • Hong Kong

Published by
World Scientific Publishing Co. Pte. Ltd.
P O Box 128, Farrer Road, Singapore 912805
USA office: Suite 1B, 1060 Main Street, River Edge, NJ 07661
UK office: 57 Shelton Street, Covent Garden, London WC2H 9HE

British Library Cataloguing-in-Publication Data
A catalogue record for this book is available from the British Library.

IMF AND THE ASIAN FINANCIAL CRISIS
Copyright © 1998 by World Scientific Publishing Co. Pte. Ltd.
All rights reserved. This book, or parts thereof, may not be reproduced in any form or by any means, electronic or mechanical, including photocopying, recording or any information storage and retrieval system now known or to be invented, without written permission from the Publisher.

For photocopying of material in this volume, please pay a copying fee through the Copyright Clearance Center, Inc., 222 Rosewood Drive, Danvers, MA 01923, USA. In this case permission to photocopy is not required from the publisher.

ISBN 981-02-3629-8

Printed in Singapore by Eurasia Press Pte Ltd

Preface

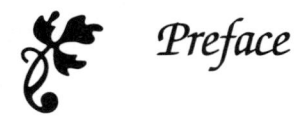

The Asian financial crisis came as a shock. The world, it seems, is neither as cosy nor as predictable as we had supposed. Despite a nation's best intentions and years of hard work, it is more evident now than ever that uninterrupted growth and prosperity can never be counted on. The value of money is merely an index of the world's confidence in a nation's economic fitness. As economic fortunes tumble, the loose change in our pockets — as has been demonstrated many times — can become worthless overnight. No wonder there remains a sense of confusion and even betrayal among many people in East Asia today — the latest victims of this apparent 'financial hegemony'. An almost dizzying succession of events of global significance (and consequence) have sprung from the financial troubles experienced by a number of Asian economies over the past 12 months. The original symptoms of disorder, which first appeared in what is (in global terms) a fairly minor South-east Asian economy, have developed into a pandemic and chronic international disease.

Though still a relatively youthful academic discipline, the power of economics in the modern world is now phenomenal. For the first time we are seeing economic dynamics acting as a correctional tool, if not a moral force, exerting influence over people's lives and behavior even where politics and religion fail to reach. Economic principles are not so tractable that they can be twisted in unnatural directions without the threat of lashing back into shape. Presidents and despots may be toppled by such mistakes; where once a certain level of corruption or even of human rights violations were seemingly acceptable, it is now revealed that a certain level of depreciation of a nation's currency is not. And while there are general rules at work that make perfect sense to everyone — both in the everyday world and in the simulatory models employed by academic economists — there are also subtle imponderables in operation. It takes more than hard work and the right economic climate to cultivate the grapes of economic prosperity; other, hazier indefinables affect the world's confidence in a nation's finances as a cloudy sky can affect the vintage.

The layman, especially a citizen of one of the afflicted countries, may be left wondering what exactly is going on. What recourse is there in such an unpredictable world? How can we prevent similar economic shocks recurring with wearying cyclical inevitability in the future? Step in, the IMF, an organization now in its 46th year, underpinned by some of the world's leading economists (though criticized by others). An International Rescue whose aid often comes at a price: financial reform, political change, fiscal tightening, and austerity measures.

A sort of natural selection is taking place: financial fitness (or frailty) is being ruthlessly exposed by internationally required standards of openness and accountability. Nations no longer find it so easy to operate according to many of their accustomed, cherished, but idiosyncratic systems. External forces in the shape of 'the market', foreign governments, and international agencies such as the IMF now all make heavy remedial demands upon individual economic systems. So who is really in control? And what of the power of those international agencies? Who, in particular, are the IMF? Where did this institution come from? Why is it necessary? What are its motives? From whence its authority? How far must its advice be followed?

Preface

With economics now asserting itself as such a correctional force in politics and society one may well be justified in asking, *quis custodes ipsos custodiet?* — whether these guardians of the world economy, functioning as a quasi-governmental force, themselves need guarding?

This book aims to introduce the IMF to the non-economist and provides a fair perspective on its increasingly significant role in world affairs. Some historical background to the IMF's inauguration and the economic context in which it operates is given, followed by a more detailed analysis of the institution's surveillance and assistance mechanisms. The development of the IMF in recent decades, especially in the light of the various economic crises it has had to deal with, is charted in Section 2, and its role in the Asian crisis is addressed in Section 3. Finally, some criticisms of the IMF, both old and new, are aired, together with some balancing counter-arguments. As both this institution and the current economic crisis in Asia (not to mention the more recent crisis in Russia) will no doubt be tenaciously featuring in our newspapers and on our television screens and radios in the near future — no matter in which country we live — such a discussion is intended to be both timely and helpful in making better sense of the modern world.

Contents

Preface	v

PART 1. WHAT IS THE IMF?

A Brief History of the IMF	1
Structure of the IMF	7
IMF and the World Bank	15

PART 2. WORKINGS OF THE IMF

IMF Surveillance	25
Financial Assistance and Conditionality	38
Indentity Crisis: The IMF in the 1970s	50
The 1980s: The Debt Crisis	58
Recent Efforts: The HIPC Initiative	66

PART 3. IMF AND THE ASIAN FINANCIAL CRISIS

IMF and the Crisis	69

IMF Programs in the Asian Crisis 76
Criticisms of the IMF 89

APPENDIX: KEY ARTICLES OF AGREEMENT OF THE IMF

Article I: Purposes 102

Article IV: Obligations Regarding Exchange Arrangements 104

Article VIII: General Obligations of Members 107

A Brief History of the IMF

The International Monetary Fund (IMF) needs no introduction. Its highly visible and sometimes contentious involvement in regional crises has attracted inordinate media attention, both positive and negative. On one end of the scale, it has been portrayed as an institutionalized financial messiah, whose mere presence alone is able to invigorate ailing economies and restore public's confidence. At the same time, it is sometimes regarded as a Western-dominated shibboleth whose measures have a placebo effect at best.

It is also commonly perceived (erroneously) as a lending institution akin to a central world bank. Such disparate opinions are, however, the result of a common want of understanding of the primary aims and functions of the IMF. Despite the Fund's international prominence and its often crucial participation in rescuing floundering economies, its exact functions and operations, its deeper economic philosophy and the specific role it plays in the international economy, remain an enigma to many. In order to be truly appreciative or critical of the Fund and its international functions, knowledge of its founding purpose and its operations in the world's economy is necessary.

So what is the IMF? It has been said that its inception would not have been possible but for 'the coincidence of the hour and of the men', that it was in many respects a fortuitous creation of circumstances and time. A brief political and economic background of the world at that particular time follows.

Of the Hour

In the absence of a common international unit of exchange, trading countries require each other's respective currencies. The present ease with which currencies are exchanged, however, belies a troubled history.

The need of the international economy to have some yardstick by which the various national currencies could be evaluated was satisfied, to some extent, by gold. Under the Gold Standard Act of 1870, the value of pound sterling was pegged to this precious metal. Other currencies were in turn fixed against the pound.

In the period leading to the Great Depression, the exchange rate of the pound proved to be unrealistic. The general economic situation — widespread unemployment and galloping inflation — caused deep fears about the worth of paper money. This gave rise to an unprecedented demand for gold far beyond that which central banks were able to supply, not least the Bank of England. In this atmosphere of economic gloom, the pound was found to be severely overvalued, affecting the British Empire's trade with the rest of the world. It was eventually forced to abandon the gold standard in 1931. Other currencies unhooked themselves from the pound and followed suit. World trade was crippled by these competitive devaluations and diminished by more than half between 1929 and 1932. Protectionism became the order of the day; high tariffs were imposed on imports, and 'export unemployment' accompanied the dramatic economic contraction. As a result, world trade came to a virtual standstill.

Furthermore, the abandonment of the gold standard by major players in the world economy left paper money in a dubious position. Not being able to gauge the value of this paper money dissuaded traders from using it, and currency exchanges between those countries

A Brief History of the IMF

which remained on the gold standard and those which did not slowed to a halt. This led to nations hoarding gold and currencies which were convertible. Exchange controls were also imposed to curtail the exchange of domestic for foreign currencies. The problem became so acute that certain trading countries even contemplated barter schemes. Moreover, economic desperation in the 1930s led other governments to deliberately devalue their national currencies in order to enhance the competitiveness of their respective exports. Consequently, this was met with retaliation in kind.

Such were the perils of an unregulated international monetary system and it was from the ashes of this demolished global economy in the 1930s that the IMF emerged.

After the bitter lessons of the two world wars, geopolitically, the world emerged from a period of isolationism. There was strong political will for establishing international organizations to rebuild the post-war world, and to work toward a new world order of political and economic co-operation on a hitherto inconceivable scale worldwide. On the economic front, this paved the way for the IMF, GATT, FAO, and the World Bank.

Of the Men

A series of unsuccessful monetary conventions which attempted to resolve the economic impasse was held. Only in the 1940s were concrete and viable proposals to reinstate economic order conceived.

In the UK, John Maynard Keynes, and in the US, Harry Dexter White envisaged permanent international financial institutions as opposed to the numerous ad hoc conventions which so characterized the 1930s, and which often had come to nothing. To deal with the related problems of competitive devaluation and protectionism which greatly emasculated world trade, any institution would possess the financial resources to support its members through the difficult periods of balance of payments deficits.

The Keynes plan, however, was more ambitious and went several steps further. Keynes proposed the creation of an international central bank, with which member states were obliged to maintain an account. It would possess the authority to create money and in this manner provide financial assistance to countries in dire straits. To prevent countries from needless devaluations, their respective exchange rates were to be fixed to an international unit of exchange called the 'bancor', which this bank would be able to issue and against which currencies of the world would be measured. Subsequent exchange rate changes would be subject to the approval of this institution in order to ensure a healthy balance of payments. Although forestalled at the inception of the IMF, the idea of the bancor was adopted in 1968 in the form of Special Drawing Rights (SDR).

In contrast, White advocated that the institution's finances be provided by contributions from member countries, and that financial assistance to troubled economies be drawn from this. It was intended that this would give the institution a more co-operative character and at the same time secure for it a greater supervisory role over a country's economic policies in order to ensure repayment.

These two suggested frameworks for international monetary systems were passionately debated during the war years. In general, it was White's plan which was eventually adopted.

Establishment

In July 1944, delegates from 45 countries convened at Bretton Woods in New Hampshire, USA, to negotiate the final provisions of the IMF charter known as the Articles of Agreement. Consensus was reached remarkably quickly and the IMF came to pass on 27 December 1945, with 29 governments ratifying the Articles of Agreement.

Not only did this 'act of faith' mark a turning point in the history of international economics, it was a beacon marking the fresh confidence of a scarred generation in working toward the building of a more peaceful and prosperous world. This is perhaps best exemplified by the partial surrender of sovereign control over economic policies, particularly in the areas of international trade and currency exchange rates. Henceforth, exchange rates were to be determined only after consultation with other member states under the auspices of the IMF.

It was felt that the enlightened intentions of the Bretton Woods conference ought to be enshrined in a code of good conduct. Articles IV and VIII of the agreement, apart from committing states to pursue sound domestic monetary and fiscal policies, also spell out the general obligations of the member states in relation to each other, specifically in the arena of international trade (see Appendix). Here, the imposition of restrictions on current payments and the manipulation of exchange rates in order to gain unfair leverage over other countries were explicitly proscribed. It was a shared experience of the member states that the period of 'competitive devaluations' of the 1930s had adverse repercussions on their respective domestic economies and that world trade as a whole had suffered.

As a result of the wild and uncontrollable fluctuations during the period leading up to the Second World War, the general feeling was that a regime of fixed exchange rate pegged to gold would be the best alternative in the promotion of world trade. Members were therefore required to establish a gold standard or a gold standard exchange and to maintain the determined rate within margins of 1% on either sides of parity. After the war, the USA maintained the price of gold at $35 to 1 ounce until 1971. The gold standard regime, coupled with the code of conduct of lifting exchange restrictions and the promotion of multilateral trade, was considered the best basis for progress in world trade and investment. This in turn could be translated into full employment and real economic growth for the member countries.

In pursuing these fundamental objectives and principles, the architects of the Fund were acutely aware of the need for financial relief in order to rectify payment imbalances. Since it was the cataclysmic disequilibrium in the balance of payments that had given rise to these crippling trading practices in the first place, it was intended that the large resources of the Fund were to be made accessible in times of payments difficulties, in order to ensure that the adherence to the code of conduct was effective.

The purposes of the IMF are described in Article I of the Articles of Agreement (see Appendix).

Structure of the IMF

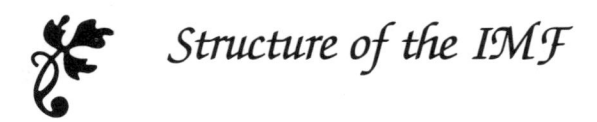

The IMF has about 2,300 staff members. Unlike the World Bank, it has no affiliates or subsidiaries. Most of its staff members are located at its Washington headquarters, although three small offices are maintained in Paris, Geneva, and at the United Nations in New York. Its professional staff members are mainly economists and financial experts.

The administration of the IMF is directly governed by the will of the member states. In other words, the Fund does not, as popular perception may assume, operate as an independent administrative body dictating economic decisions and instructions to its members. Rather, it is the members themselves who are ultimately in control of decision-making. The Fund thus acts only as an intermediary between the will of the majority of the membership and the individual member country. This arrangement is apparent from the constitution and structure of the organisation (see Chart on page 8).

Board of Governors

At the apex of the hierarchy sits the Board of Governors, composed of one representative from each member state. In addition, there is

Organization Chart

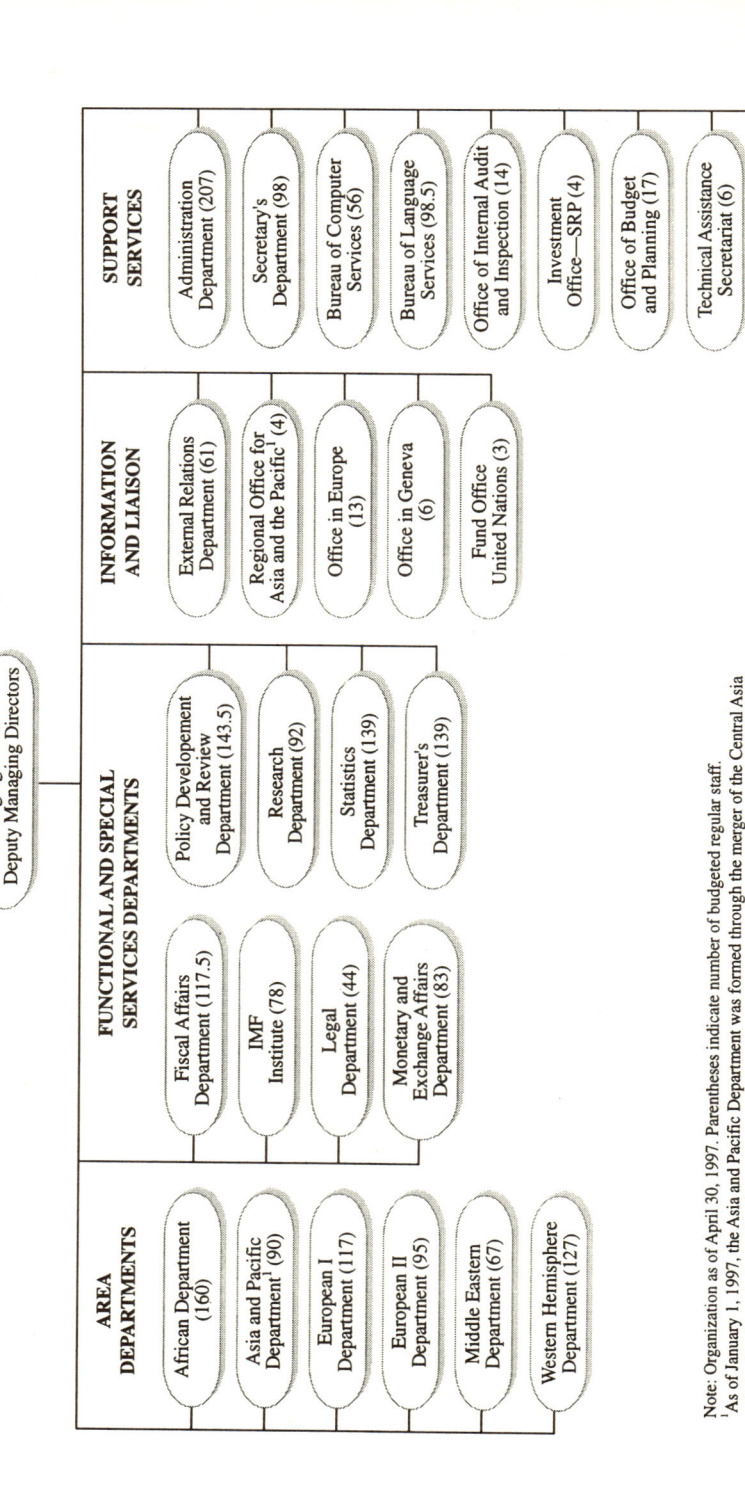

- Board of Governors
- Executive Board
- Managing Director / Deputy Managing Directors

AREA DEPARTMENTS
- African Department (160)
- Asia and Pacific Department[1] (90)
- European I Department (117)
- European II Department (95)
- Middle Eastern Department (67)
- Western Hemisphere Department (127)

FUNCTIONAL AND SPECIAL SERVICES DEPARTMENTS
- Fiscal Affairs Department (117.5)
- IMF Institute (78)
- Legal Department (44)
- Monetary and Exchange Affairs Department (83)
- Policy Developement and Review Department (143.5)
- Research Department (92)
- Statistics Department (139)
- Treasurer's Department (139)

INFORMATION AND LIAISON
- External Relations Department (61)
- Regional Office for Asia and the Pacific[1] (4)
- Office in Europe (13)
- Office in Geneva (6)
- Fund Office United Nations (3)

SUPPORT SERVICES
- Administration Department (207)
- Secretary's Department (98)
- Bureau of Computer Services (56)
- Bureau of Language Services (98.5)
- Office of Internal Audit and Inspection (14)
- Investment Office—SRP (4)
- Office of Budget and Planning (17)
- Technical Assistance Secretariat (6)
- Work Practices and Technology Secretariat[2] (3)

Note: Organization as of April 30, 1997. Parentheses indicate number of budgeted regular staff.

[1] As of January 1, 1997, the Asia and Pacific Department was formed through the merger of the Central Asia and the Southeast Asia and Pacific Departments.
The Regional Office for Asia and the Pacific was also established on this date.

[2] Effective May 1, 1997, the Work Practices and Technology Secretariat was transferred to the Office of Internal Audit and Inspection and redesignated as the Work Practices Section.

also an equal number of Alternate Governors. Both Governors and Alternate Governors are almost invariably ministers of finance or heads of central banks from their respective countries, and therefore speak authoritatively for their governments. The Board convenes only during annual meetings for the administration of IMF matters, taking into account the commitments and responsibilities each representative has already in his own country. However, between annual meetings, a Governor may take votes by mail or other means. Assisting in the decision-making process of the Board are the Interim Committee and a joint IMF/World Bank Development Committee. The former provides general advice on the functioning of the international monetary system, whilst the latter advises on the special needs of poorer countries.

Executive Board

At the second tier in the IMF's chain of command is the Executive Board. Many of the Executive Board's duties are delegated from the Board of Governors, and it is responsible for overseeing the everyday operations of the Fund. There are 24 Executive Directors, eight of whom represent the individual countries of China, France, Germany, Japan, Russia, Saudi Arabia, the United Kingdom, and the United States. The rest are regional representatives of the remaining countries. The Executive Board acts as a liaison body between the IMF and the individual Governors during the rest of the year when the Board of Governors are not meeting. Governors communicate their respective countries' agendas to the Executive Board which will then, convening at least three times a week in formal session, supervise the implementation of related policies. Country-specific policies are thus often handled at this level. Each Executive Director wields a certain number of votes, largely in proportion to the contribution of the member state being represented. However, in making decisions, the Executive Board rarely resorts to the process of formal voting but relies on the formation of consensus among its members.

IMF Staff

The Chairman of the Executive Board, appointed by the Board of Governors on a five-year renewable term, is also the Managing Director of the IMF, and heads the rest of the 2,300 strong staff. The staff is largely comprised of economists, statisticians, research scholars, experts in public finance and taxation, linguists, writers, and support personnel from around the world. Roughly a quarter of these deal directly with its membership on a jurisdictional basis and another quarter deal with overall Fund concerns on a functional basis.

Jurisdiction is divided along five quasi-continental areas: Africa, Asia, Europe, the Middle East and the Western Hemisphere. Areas of functional speciality include: Legal, Central Banking, Fiscal Affairs (FAD), Exchange and Trade Relations (ETR), and the Research and Treasurer's Departments. Other staff fill a variety of support and administrative functions. Finally, there are also independent international civil servants not representing national interests.

Membership

IMF membership is open to every country that conducts its own foreign policy and is willing to adhere to the IMF charter of rights and obligations. All major countries are now members of the Fund, and at the last count, the membership roster numbered 182 countries. Members can of course leave the Fund on the same voluntary basis upon which they joined.

The implication of joining the IMF is that a member country undertakes to cooperate in the furtherance of the Fund's goals. This includes the obligation to maintain transparency in its arrangements for determining the value of its currency in relation to the currency of other countries; to refrain from restricting the exchange of its currency for foreign currency; and to pursue sound economic policies that will be constructively beneficial for both its own national wealth and that of the whole membership. While the IMF, being a voluntary institution, has no powers to force compliance upon its members, substantial moral pressure can be asserted, given the IMF's international standing.

By a majority of its members, the IMF may also deny an offending member from eligibility from borrowing money or even evict a member from the organization. These are of course last-resort measures. Consistent with the nature and disposition of an organization of mutual consent, a sympathetic position is normally taken toward a member who lapses in fulfilling the obligations as result of factors beyond the member's immediate control.

Quota Subscriptions

It is a condition upon entry into the IMF that each member has to contribute a certain amount of money to the organization. This contribution is known as a 'quota subscription', because it translates into the quota which has been assigned to the member. A quota is designed broadly to reflect the size and strength of the member's economy, and is a device used to define a member's financial and organizational relations with the IMF.

The quota serves a variety of purposes. Most apparently, the subscription money itself forms part of the IMF funds from which fiscal lending to members in economic difficulty is drawn. As a functional corollary to this, quotas determine the cumulative amount of outstanding loan members can have with the Fund at any one time. Additionally, the periodic allocations to members of the IMF's special assets known as SDRs (special drawing rights) is also determined by quotas. The more a member contributes, the greater the allocation to which it is entitled. Finally, quotas determine the voting power of members. Each member has 250 votes plus one additional vote for each SDR 100,000 of its quota (see Box).

As required by the IMF's Articles of Agreement, quotas are reviewed not more than every five years and they are frequently adjusted to reflect the expansion in the world economy or changes in the individual economies of the member states. A member is generally required to pay up to 25% of its quota subscription in SDRs or in the currencies of other members specified by the IMF. The remainder is paid in that country's own currency.

What are SDRs?

One of the IMF's roles is to supervise the international supply of liquidity. For that purpose, special drawing rights (SDRs) were created by the Fund under the First Amendment to its Articles of Agreement. If the members consider that there is a danger of a shortage of international liquidity, the Fund can issue SDRs to supplement the existing official reserves of member countries.

In conducting international trade, countries need to maintain prudent amounts of reserve assets in foreign currencies and gold in order to pay off their debts. SDRs are meant to be treated as part of these reserve assets, and serve as a reliable and universally recognized source of currency to facilitate payments that have to be settled in foreign exchange. SDRs may be used in transactions and operations between member countries, with 15 other 'prescribed institutional holders', and with the IMF itself. Certain member countries may also be designated by the IMF to provide freely usable currency in exchange for SDRs from all other member countries, thus adding to the facilitation of international exchange. These members' obligations to provide currency is limited to its holding of SDRs not exceeding three times its net cumulative allocation, although the IMF and the member may agree on a higher limit.

The value of and interest on this international reserve asset is based on the average worth of the world's five major currencies: the U.S. dollar, Deutschemark, Japanese yen, French franc and pound sterling. This SDR valuation basket is revised every five years with modifications made to the weightings attached to each currency in order to reflect changes in their relative value in international trade and reserves. Also, since the movement in the exchange rate of any one component currency will tend to be partly or fully offset by movements in the exchange rates of the other currencies, a further measure of stability in the value of the SDR is ensured. In fact, as of 30 April 1997, the currencies of two member countries were pegged to the SDR. As for the SDR interest rate, which is adjusted weekly, it is based on a weighted average of the yields on specified short-term instruments in the domestic markets of the five countries. At present, these instruments are the market yield on three-month U.S. treasury bills; the three-month German interbank deposit rate; the three-month rate on Japanese certificates of deposit; the three-month rate on French treasury bills; and the market yield on three-month UK treasury bills.

Today, there are 21.4 billion SDRs in existence, accounting for about 2% of all non-gold reserves. However, the success of the SDR in relieving international illiquidity has been somewhat limited. There has been insufficient agreement on the need for further SDR allocations, owing to the proliferation of international financial markets where many countries can easily supplement their official reserves.

Areas of Activity

The most important role of the Fund is that of a manager of an orderly, predictable and stable international monetary system with open borders, providing a framework for world trade and the economies of the member states. To this end, the IMF resorts to three primary functions; surveillance of the monetary system and exchange rate policy of member states, granting credit to countries with balance of payments difficulties, and providing policy recommendations to members.

Surveillance is the process by which the IMF appraises its members' exchange rate policies within the framework of a comprehensive analysis of the general economic situation and the policy strategy of each member. The IMF fulfills its surveillance responsibilities through: annual bilateral Article IV consultations with individual countries; multilateral surveillance twice a year in the context of its World Economic Outlook exercise; and precautionary arrangements, enhanced surveillance, and program monitoring, which provide a member with close monitoring from the IMF in the absence of the use of Fund resources.

Financial assistance provided with a view toward maintaining stability within the global economy is also of paramount importance. Credits and loans may be extended by the IMF to member countries with balance of payments problems, or to support policies of adjustment and reform.

Finally, the IMF offers technical assistance consisting of expertise and aid in several broad areas: the design and implementation of fiscal and monetary policy; institution-building (such as the development of central banks or treasuries); handling and accounting of transactions with the IMF and, together with other international financial organisations, through the Joint Vienna Institute.

IMF and the World Bank

Many people have difficulty in telling the IMF and the World Bank apart. Even John Maynard Keynes, a founding father of both institutions, once said at the inaugural meeting of the IMF that he was confused by the names. He thought the Fund should be called a bank, and the Bank should be called a fund.

At first glance, the Bank and the IMF appear quite similar. Both are in a sense owned and directed by the governments of member nations. In addition, both institutions deal extensively with economic issues and direct their efforts at broadening and strengthening the economies of their member nations. Staff members of both the Bank and IMF often appear at international conventions, speaking the same arcane language of the economics and development experts.

The two institutions hold joint annual meetings, and are often reported in the media to be negotiating involved programs of economic adjustment with ministers of finance or other government officials. Both have headquarters in Washington, DC and share a library and other facilities. Both exchange economic information regularly, present joint seminars, hold informal meetings, and occasionally send out joint missions to member nations.

Despite these similarities the two institutions are in fact quite distinct, being set up for different purposes. They are funded from different sources, they assist different categories of members, and each institution strives to achieve distinct goals through methods peculiar to itself. But the most essential difference is this: the World Bank is primarily a development institution; while the IMF is a cooperative institution that seeks to maintain an orderly system of payments and receipts between nations, so as to promote and maintain the international monetary system.

As described earlier, the IMF was set up in reaction to the financial problems initiating and protracting the Great Depression of the 1930s: sudden, unpredictable variations in the exchange values of national currencies and a widespread disinclination among governments to allow their national currencies to be exchanged for foreign currencies.

The IMF's main concern therefore remains the health of the world's trade and financial systems. Established as a voluntary and cooperative institution, it requires its member nations to relinquish some measure of national sovereignty by abjuring practices injurious to the economic welfare of their fellow member nations.

The World Bank, on the other hand, is a development organization — hence its official name of 'International Bank for Reconstruction and Development' (IBRD). At Bretton Woods the international community assigned the aims of financing economic development to the World Bank. The Bank's first loans were extended during the late 1940s to finance the reconstruction of the war-ravaged economies of Western Europe. When these nations recovered some measure of economic self-sufficiency, the Bank turned its attention to assisting the world's poorer nations, known as developing countries, to which it has loaned more than $330 billion since the 1940s. Its mandated goal is to 'reduce poverty and improve living standards by promoting sustainable growth and investment in people'. In recent years the Bank has confirmed its main aim to be 'substantial poverty reduction'.

The rules of the institution, contained in the IMF's Articles of Agreement, constitute a code of conduct. The code is simple: it requires members to allow their currencies to be exchanged for foreign currencies freely and without restriction; to keep the IMF informed of changes they contemplate in financial and monetary policies that will affect fellow members' economies; and, as far as possible, to modify these policies on the advice of the IMF in order to accommodate the needs of the entire membership. To help nations abide by the code of conduct, the IMF governs a pool of money from which members can borrow when the need arises. The IMF is not, however, a lender of last-resort funds that can create new forms of liquidity, as is the Bank. It is first and foremost an overseer of its members' monetary and exchange rate policies and a guardian of the code of conduct. The IMF's *raison d'être* is to provide an orderly monetary system that will encourage trade and create jobs.

Philosophically committed to the orderly and stable growth of the world economy, the IMF seeks to avoid surprises. It receives frequent reports on members' economic policies and prospects, which it debates, comments on, and communicates to the entire membership so that other members may respond with full knowledge of the facts and a clear understanding of how their own domestic policies might be affected.

The structure of the World Bank is more intricate. The Bank comprises two major organizations: the International Bank for Reconstruction and Development, and the International Development Association (IDA). Its affiliations and subsidiaries include the International Finance Corporation — which mobilizes funding for private enterprises in developing countries — the International Centre for Settlement of Investment Disputes, and the Multilateral Guarantee Agency.

With over 7,000 staff members, the World Bank Group is around three times the size of the IMF, and maintains about 40 offices throughout the world although 95% of its staff work at its Washington, DC headquarters.

The Bank employs staff with a wide range of expertise: economists, engineers, urban planners, agronomists, statisticians, lawyers, portfolio managers, loan officers, project appraisers, as well as experts in telecommunications, water supply and sewerage, transportation, education, energy, rural development, population and health care, and other disciplines.

Sources of Funding

The World Bank is an investment bank, mediating between investors and recipients, borrowing from one and lending to the other. Its owners are the governments of its 180 member nations with equity shares in the Bank — valued at about $176 billion in June 1995.

The IBRD obtains most of the development-financing funds it lends by market borrowing through the issue of bonds to individuals and private institutions in more than 100 countries. The bonds carry an AAA rating because repayment is guaranteed by member governments. Its concessional loan associate, the IDA, is largely financed by grants from donor nations. The Bank is a major borrower in the world's capital markets and the largest non-resident borrower in virtually all countries where its issues are sold. It also borrows money by selling bonds and notes directly to governments, their agencies, and central banks. The proceeds of these bond sales are in turn lent to developing countries at affordable rates of interest to help finance projects and policy reform programs.

The IMF, on the other hand, is not a bank and does not intermediate between investors and recipients. It is more like a credit union whose members have access to a common pool of resources. Presently valued at over $215 billion, these resources come from quota subscriptions, or membership fees, paid by the IMF's 182 member countries. Each member contributes a certain amount of money proportionate to its economic size and strength to this pool of resources (richer countries pay more, poorer less). Although the IMF borrows from official entities under special and highly restrictive circumstances, it relies mainly on its quota subscriptions to finance its operations. The adequacy of these resources is reviewed every five years.

Recipients of Funding

Neither wealthy countries nor private individuals borrow from the World Bank, which lends only to creditworthy governments of developing nations. Those countries whose per capita gross national product (GNP) exceeds $1,305 may borrow from the IBRD. These loans carry an interest rate slightly above the market rate at which the Bank itself borrows, and must generally be repaid within 12–15 years. The IDA, on the other hand, lends only to governments of developing nations whose per capita GNP is below $1,305. In practice, IDA loans frequently go to countries with annual per capita incomes below $865. IDA loans are interest free and have a maturity of 35 or 40 years.

In contrast, all member nations of IMF, both wealthy and poor, have the right to financial assistance from the IMF. Maintaining an orderly and stable international monetary system requires all participants in that system to fulfil their financial obligations to other participants. Membership of the IMF gives to each country that experiences a shortage of foreign exchange (regardless of economic size or per capita GNP) *temporary access to the pool of currencies* to resolve this difficulty, usually referred to as a balance of payments problem. Money received from the IMF must normally be repaid within three to five years, and in no case later than ten years. Interest rates are slightly below market rates, but are not as concessional as those assigned to the World Bank's IDA loans.

Operations

The World Bank exists to encourage poor countries to develop by providing them with technical assistance and funding for projects and policies that will realize the countries' economic potential. The Bank views development as a long-term, integrated endeavor and provides most of its financial and technical assistance to developing countries by supporting specific projects.

During the first two decades of its existence, two-thirds of the assistance provided by the Bank went to electric power and transportation projects. The Bank has diversified its activities in recent years, and now gives particular attention to projects that directly benefit the poorest people in developing countries through loans for agriculture and rural development, small-scale enterprises, and urban development. Such projects help in giving access to safe water, waste-disposal facilities, health care, family-planning assistance, nutrition, education, and housing. Transportation projects often give attention to the construction of farm-to-market roads; power projects increasingly provide lighting and power for villages and small farms; and industrial projects place greater emphasis on creating jobs in small enterprises. Labor-intensive construction is used where practicable. In addition to electric power, the Bank is active in supporting development of oil, gas, coal, wood, and biomass as alternative sources of energy. The decision on whether a project will receive IBRD or IDA financing depends on the economic conditions of the country and not on the characteristics of the project.

The Bank also serves as executing agency for technical assistance projects financed by the United Nations Development Program in agriculture and rural development, energy, and economic planning. In response to the economic climate in many of its member countries, the Bank is now emphasizing technical assistance for institutional development and macroeconomic policy formulation.

Every project supported by the Bank is designed in close collaboration with national governments and local agencies, and often in cooperation with other multilateral assistance organizations. In making loans to developing countries, the Bank does not compete with other sources of finance. It assists only those projects for which the required capital is not available from other sources on reasonable terms. Through its work, the Bank seeks to strengthen the economies of borrowing nations so that they can graduate from reliance on Bank resources and meet their own financial needs, on terms they can afford from conventional sources of capital.

The range of the Bank's activities is far broader than its lending operations. Since the Bank's lending decisions depend heavily on the economic conditions in the borrowing countries, the Bank makes careful studies of these economies and the needs of the sectors for which lending is contemplated. These analyses help in formulating an appropriate long-term development assistance strategy for that economy.

Successful graduation from the IBRD and IDA to alternative sources of funding has indeed taken place over the years. Of the 34 very poor countries that borrowed money from the IDA during the earliest years, more than two dozen have made enough progress that they no longer need IDA money, leaving that money available to other countries who joined the Bank more recently. Similarly, about 20 countries that formerly borrowed money from the IBRD no longer have to do so.

The IMF has gone through two distinct phases in its 50-year history. During the first phase, ending in 1973, the institution oversaw the adoption of general convertibility among the major currencies, and supervised a system of fixed exchange rates tied to the value of gold. Difficulties encountered in maintaining a system of fixed exchange rates gave rise to unstable monetary and financial conditions throughout the world and led the international community to reconsider how the IMF could most effectively function in a regime of flexible exchange rates. After five years of analysis and negotiation (1973–78), the second phase began with the amendment of the IMF's constitution in 1978, broadening its functions to enable it to grapple with the challenges that had arisen since the collapse of the 'par value' system. Its functions now include:

1. Urging its members to allow their national currencies to be exchanged without restriction for the currencies of other member countries.
2. Supervising economic policies that influence members' balance of payments in the presently legalized flexible exchange rate environment. This supervision provides opportunities for an early warning of any exchange rate or balance of payments problem. In this, the IMF's role is mainly advisory. It confers at regular intervals (usually once a year) with its members, analyzing their economic positions and apprising them of actual or potential problems arising from their policies, and keeps the entire membership informed of these developments.
3. Continuing to provide short- and medium-term financial assistance to member nations that run into temporary balance of payments difficulties. The financial assistance usually involves the provision by the IMF of convertible currencies to augment the afflicted member's dwindling foreign exchange reserves, but only in return for the government's promise to reform the economic policies that caused the balance of payments problem in the first place.

The IMF sees its financial role in these cases not as subsidizing further deficits but as facilitating a country's painful transition to living within its means.

The key which opens the door to IMF assistance is the member's balance of payments (the tally of its payments and receipts with other nations). Foreign payments should be in approximate balance; a country should bring in approximately what it pays out. When financial problems cause the value of a member's currency and the price of its goods to fall out of line, balance of payments difficulties are the inevitable result. If this happens, the member country may, by virtue of the Articles of Agreement, apply to the IMF for assistance.

In a collaborative effort, the country and the IMF can then attempt to root out the causes of the payments imbalance by creating a comprehensive program to reorganize the economy. Because doing so is often disruptive and costly, the IMF will lend money to subsidize policy reforms during the period of transition. To ensure that this money is used productively, the IMF closely monitors the country's economic progress during this time, providing technical assistance and further consultative services as needed.

Over the past few years, the IMF has been strengthening its supervision of members' economic policies in response to a growing keenness of the world community to return to a more stable system of exchange rates and reduce the present fluctuations in the currency values. Provisions exist in its Articles of Agreement that would allow the IMF to adopt a more active role should the world community opt for stricter management of flexible exchange rates or even for a return to some system of stable exchange rates.

The IMF is also authorized to issue a special type of money, called the SDR (Special Drawing Rights), to provide its members with additional liquidity. Known technically as a fiduciary asset, the SDR may be retained by members as part of their monetary reserves or be used in place of national currencies in transactions with other members. To date the IMF has issued slightly over 21.4 billion SDRs, presently valued at about $30 billion.

Cooperation between the World Bank and the IMF

Although the Bank and the IMF are independent entities, they have worked together in close cooperation on numerous occasions. Focusing on structural reform in recent years has resulted in a considerable convergence of the efforts of the Bank and the IMF, leading them to greater reliance on each other's special expertise. This convergence has been hastened by the debt crisis — a result of the inability of developing countries to repay the enormous loans they contracted during the late 1970s and early 1980s. The debt crisis has highlighted the fact that economic growth can be sustained only when resources are being used efficiently, and that this can only take place in the context of a stable monetary and financial environment.

The foundations of the cooperation between the Bank and the IMF are in the form of regular and frequent interaction between economists and loan officers who work in the same country. To this cooperation the Bank staff brings a longer-term view of the slow process of development, and a profound knowledge of the structural requirements and economic potential of a particular country. The IMF staff contributes its own perspective on the day-to-day capability of a country to sustain its flow of payments to creditors, and its ability to attract investment finance, as well as on how the country is integrated within the world economy.

This interchange of information is backed up by the coordination of financial assistance to each other's members. In addition, both institutions encourage other lenders, both private and official, to join them in co-financing projects and in mobilizing credits to countries that are in need. Cooperation between the Bretton Woods Institutions has resulted in the identification of programs that will encourage growth in a stable economic environment and in the coordination of financing which will ensure the success of these programs. Devising programs in the future that will integrate members' economies more fully into the international monetary and financial system, and at the same time encourage economic expansion, continues to challenge the expertise of both institutions.

References

The IMF home page: http://www.imf.org/.

IMF Surveillance

The 'par value' system was to an extent self-enforcing and required minimal supervision. Since the demise of this system in the 1970s (making way for various other methods of determining the exchange value of currencies) the IMF has had to be even more deeply involved in monitoring aspects of its members' economies which have a bearing on the exchange value of currencies. The challenge was to penetrate beyond exchange values and into a critical evaluation of the range of economic policies which influence them. This activity has come to be known as surveillance.

Surveillance naturally calls for greater transparency of members' policies as well as a greater scope of IMF inquiry into individual economies. The justification for such supervision is based on the conviction that strong and consistent domestic economic policies will lead to stable exchange rates which in turn affect the growth and prosperity of the global economy. This position, reinforcing the notion that exchange among national currencies is still very much within the domain of international interest, was ratified in an amendment to the Articles of Agreement that called for the IMF to 'exercise firm surveillance over the exchange rate policies of members'. Increasingly, over the years, surveillance has evolved to become the vehicle by which the exercise of discretion is monitored, and one of the Fund's most significant responsibilities.

The IMF carries out its surveillance responsibilities mainly through regular Article IV consultations with member countries and through multilateral discussions held in the context of the Executive Board's twice-yearly World Economic Outlook reviews.

The Scope of Surveillance

Not surprisingly, exposing domestic policies to global scrutiny can be a sensitive issue. The focus of surveillance therefore must center itself only on the points and the terms of convergence between national economies. Policies devoid of international repercussions fall outside the sphere of surveillance. Broadly speaking, surveillance involves itself mostly with issues concerning the balance of payments, exchange rates, and the exchange system.

In a system where members adopt the exchange arrangement of their choice, the concept of an appropriate balance of payments position is not easy to define operationally. From an institutional standpoint, the closest to an appropriate definition of balance of payments equilibrium would be a sustainable external payments position at a realistic exchange rate in a setting free of exchange and trade restrictions. It is quite apparent that the application of such a definition is fraught with operational difficulties, since the terms 'sustainable' and 'realistic' require value-laden judgements. The relevant notion of sustainability, or viability, of the external payments position also implies a time framework, usually over a prolonged period. If external imbalance means that the balance of payments has reached a clearly unsustainable position, then the focus of policy must be on restoring viability to the balance of payments over the medium term. This concept includes objectives such as a sound growth rate and relatively stable price performance. This means that wider issues must inevitably be incorporated within the IMF's final analysis. It should be added that the evaluation of the soundness of the balance of payments position is not only in regard to the economy's overall external payments position, but also to the appropriateness of the structure of those payments. The latter asks the question of whether the global external constraint is being respected. Such a judgement requires in-depth analysis of the current account balance, capital flows, and international reserve management. In turn, these require the formulation of views on the exchange rate and the exchange system. Thus, it can be seen that although the focus of surveillance is on external economic variables, because of the nature of the required assessments, its scope must extend beyond those variables into a complex and inseparable web of internal factors as well.

Another difficult issue that compounds the problem relating to the scope of the Fund's surveillance responsibility is the fact that no definite frontier distinguishing the external from the internal dimensions of an economy can be readily discerned. The ambiguity is such that one might not be aware of the degree of incursion into the domestic sphere which will occur, when considering the viability or appropriateness of an external payments position.

The scope of surveillance therefore becomes very much a matter of degree, and the task is to identify prominent areas of domestic policy that can properly be said to influence, primarily, the economy's external position. Once a basis for general consensus among the membership can be established as to what these areas are, international scrutiny will be given the mark of legitimacy. Over time, the IMF has developed such a consensus amongst its members about key areas for international policy surveillance. The focus of the discussion that follows will seek to trace the evolution and current status of that consensus.

Through its early experience, the IMF has recognized the interdependence between the balance of payments, the exchange rate, and the exchange system, on the one hand, and the stance of macroeconomic policy or aggregate demand management on the other.

Accordingly, member countries have long endorsed the need for the IMF, in its exercise of surveillance, to appraise the appropriateness of domestic fiscal and monetary policies. In fact, during the period of the Bretton Woods order, a conventional but important distinction was drawn on what could be termed stabilization (which fell within the purview of the IMF) and development (which represented the domain of the World Bank). Broad classifications along economic policy lines were based on this distinction, and it could often be heard that in dealing with stabilization problems, the IMF focused on macroeconomic, or aggregate demand management; while in contrast the World Bank — interested mainly in development issues — tended to concentrate on microeconomic, or aggregate supply and production management. But economic concepts seldom stand in isolation, and the distinction between the institutional domains could not be so rigid. Microeconomics and supply responses affected the process of stabilization just as much as macroeconomic and aggregate demand influenced the process of development. Since the concepts are not mutually exclusive it is not surprising that there are areas of overlap in the economic duties of the two organizations. Clearly, this problem would have affected the scope of surveillance by the IMF.

Broadly speaking, however, the distinction of institutional responsibilities generally reflected the evolution of the international economy during the Bretton Woods period. A strong case can be made that the rules prevailing with the par value system helped identify the extent to which domestic policies conflicted with members' international commitments, thus also helping to identify the boundaries of institutional responsibility. The shift from policy rules to policy discretion that followed the Bretton Woods order affected the links between the domestic and external economic policy domains, bringing to the forefront the question of the appropriate boundaries for institutional action. In this process, the existing understandings concerning institutional policy assignments and responsibilities were inevitably influenced.

New distinctions were introduced to supplement or replace old ones. In the IMF, the emphasis moved from stabilization toward adjustment, which encompassed the features of stabilization but went beyond it by reaching into the structure of the economy. In the World Bank, although development retained its importance, attention moved toward so-called structural adjustment. While containing some of the aspects of development, structural adjustment reached back into the broad policy environment in the economy and thus seemed to include some elements that were prerequisites for development. In fact, it very much appeared as if the process of economic evolution encompassed a number of successive and progressively complex phases: stabilization, adjustment, structural adjustment, development, and growth. Institutionally, the specific roles coalesced toward stabilization-cum-adjustment for the IMF and development-cum-structural reform for the Bank. An overlapping interest in structural adjustment and growth developed as both of them, it could be claimed, had a bearing on the balance of payments and investment flows. The areas of common interest became even more apparent with the development of external debt strategy, in which structural adjustment, reform, and growth acquired particular importance.

Not too distant events in the international economy have paved the way for a new subject of interest, which may be called the economics of reform. This includes the efforts of a number of Central and Eastern European countries as well as the former Soviet republics to move their economies from central planning to market-based systems. The subject raises a question regarding the role of surveillance in the context of reform, particularly since the international community most assuredly has an interest in the effectiveness of the process underway. Surveillance and reform share compatible aims: the purpose of reforms is to set the conditions for the establishment of free market economies, and the purpose of surveillance is to foster norms of behavior based on freedom of international transactions among member economies as a means of enhancing their common welfare. Briefly, two dimensions of surveillance acquire particular importance for the reforming economies. The immediate one is the policy advice involved in the exercise of surveillance — this can assist the economies in laying the groundwork for the establishment of a market. The other relevant dimension is to 'preach by example'. Successful surveillance within the membership resulting in a flourishing international market can only encourage the reforming economies to keep their markets open in a similar way and abide by market discipline.

Even if there is a consensus that economic surveillance should properly focus on external variables, its practical implementation requires paying attention to domestic policies. Therefore, surveillance is unlikely ever to become a straightforward exercise. Its complexity derives from the close interdependence of economic policies, both nationally and internationally, and it calls for increasingly fine judgements in drawing the boundaries between national and international domains.

Evolving Issues

The following issues in surveillance have gained prominence in recent years:

Strengthening banking systems. Since 1980, roughly two-thirds of the IMF member countries have had problems in their banking sectors, with many bank failures having international repercussions. At a meeting in March 1997, the Executive Directors agreed that the IMF should play an important role in international efforts to promote sound banking principles and practices worldwide. In its exercise of surveillance, the IMF can help to encourage members to adopt guidelines and standards developed by the supervisory committee and then monitor their progress. The Fund has called for close collaboration in these efforts with other organizations — including the World Bank and the Basle Committee on Banking Supervision — to ensure that each focuses on its area of comparative advantage and to avoid any potential conflict in standards. In this context, the IMF will help disseminate the Basle Committee's recently published 'core principles' for effective banking among its members through surveillance (and technical assistance).

Capital account convertibility. The movement of capital among countries is a central concern of the IMF, since an open and liberal system of capital movement fosters economic growth and prosperity by contributing to an efficient allocation of world savings and investment. During meetings in February and April 1997, the Executive Board agreed that capital account liberalization should be an orderly and sustainable process and part of a broad and well-sequenced reform effort involving sound macroeconomic policies and strong financial systems. Although the absence of a formal mandate has not prevented the IMF from playing an important role in supporting members' efforts toward liberalization and monitoring international capital flows, most Directors supported an amendment of the IMF Articles of Agreement making the promotion of capital account liberalization a specific object of the IMF and to give it jurisdiction over capital movements.

Governance. Good governance has come to be widely recognized as essential for economic efficiency and growth. Governance essentially involves the implementation by a responsible government of sound and consistent economic policies. Aspects of governance that are of particular relevance to the IMF arise principally in two spheres: that of improving the management of public resources through reforms covering public sector institutions (such as the treasury, central bank and public enterprises), and by supporting the development and maintenance of a transparent and stable economic and regulatory environment conducive to efficient private sector activities (eg. price systems and exchange and trade regimes). Reflecting the increased significance that member countries attach to the promotion of good governance, the Executive Board held discussions on the role of the IMF in governance issues in January and May 1997. In July, the Board released guidelines on governance for IMF staff, which seek to strengthen the Fund's involvement in governance issues, in particular through:

- more comprehensive treatment in the context of Article IV consultations and IMF-supported programs of those governance issues that are within the IMF's mandate and expertise and that have significant macroeconomic implications;
- a more proactive approach in advocating institutions and systems that aim to eliminate corruption and other fraudulent activity; and
- enhanced collaboration with other multilateral institutions.

Fundamental Principles of Operation

There are three essential principles in the operating methods of the IMF, supplemented by a fourth that lends a pragmatic edge to their application. There is, first, the principle of *universality*, according to which IMF membership is all-encompassing and does not normally establish distinctions among countries or groups of countries. Closely connected to this is the principle of *uniformity of treatment*, according to which the IMF is expected to act without discrimination: Treatment of members must remain equal and comparable, allowing for no preferences in favor of any country or group of countries. However, it would be a mistaken view if uniformity is taken to mean the provision of equal treatment regardless of circumstances; on the contrary, for uniformity to operate in an unequal world, there must be provisions for allowing the prevailing unequal circumstances to be taken into account. This is again an exercise of judgement on the part of the IMF. The third basic principle is political *neutrality*, which aims at keeping the attention of the IMF focused on international issues. It calls for a permanent effort to maintain an appropriate balance between the interests of individual members and those of the membership as a whole.

The actual application of these principles is tempered in practice by the exercise of discretion. Such latitude is allowed for by the fourth principle of operation of the IMF, which is *flexibility* in its relations with members. When decision-making is attempted in an international forum, a plethora of problems can arise if one is blind to the peculiar circumstances confronting each individual country. Faced with this difficulty, the singular challenge for the IMF has been its ability to avert a conflict of its basic operational principles with the diversity that prevails among countries. An appropriate mix of flexibility — sensitivity to a particular member's circumstances — with universality, uniformity and neutrality — the common aspects of every membership — is thus required for a sustained balance between national and international interests.

Acknowledgment of Diversity

As alluded to above, reality precludes the application of the principle of uniformity in an absolute sense. The principle of flexibility requires that the IMF acknowledges the vast differences between countries — wide economic gulfs in particular — and takes these differences on board in formulating equitable policies. At the same time, this issue is also addressed in the administrative structure of the IMF, where differences in economic power are accounted for by the allocation of different weights to members. Member countries, for example, have different quotas (subscriptions) and voting powers commensurate with their economic strength.

From the standpoint of surveillance, a number of inferences can be drawn from the diversity recognized within the membership. A clear responsibility of all members, regardless of their individual weights within the institution, is to observe the commitments they undertake in subscribing to the code of conduct. This is equivalent to keeping their own economies in good order and in line with the prescription of the Articles of Agreement. Yet the very acceptance of differences among economies carries as a corollary the acknowledgement that the scope and influence of national economic policies also vary.

For countries with economies relatively small in size, the international environment in which they operate may be considered exogenous. The essence of their commitment is to keep balance in their own economies and respect the code of conduct. Surveillance in these cases appraises the appropriateness of domestic economic policies — that is, it assesses the individual country's observance of the rules of the game in the context of the existing external environment.

Even (or especially) for countries with relatively large economies, the international setting cannot be considered as a given, immovable ambient. On the contrary, the external environment reflects to a significant extent the national economic policy decisions which those countries make. The nature of their international commitment, therefore, must include concern for the consequences of their actions in relation to the system at large. Beyond assessing the appropriateness of national policies in isolation, the exercise of surveillance must encompass consideration of the extent to which those policies contribute to a stable international setting.

There is, then, a fundamental rationale for the establishment of differentiation in the exercise of surveillance. Indeed, such differentiation is necessary to ensure both symmetry and uniformity of treatment among members. This is yet another example of the fact that realistic acknowledgement of inequality can be the best means for dispensing equality.

A Multilateral Exercise

The exercise of surveillance has tended to be country-specific, whereby individual member countries are supervised in isolation. Although surveillance does involve the entire membership during discussions at the Executive Board level, the bulk of the operation has tended to be based almost exclusively on discussions between the IMF and each individual member. This was because during the Bretton Woods period, observance of the rules broadly ensured the stability of the system as a whole. Accordingly, no particular emphasis had to be given explicitly to systemic considerations — except, of course, for such global issues as the adequacy of international liquidity. At that time, bilateral consultations between the IMF and each country constituted the central instrument of surveillance.

The move to the current regime, by which members can opt for the exchange arrangements of their choice, provided less assurance that such bilateral consultations, focusing only on individual members policies, would be sufficient to ensure stability to the global economic environment. The effects of national policies on the international economy, as well as the consequences of interdependence among those national policies, began to receive increasing attention. As a result, the scope of bilateral discussions with large countries was broadened to explicitly include international aspects in the annual consultations. Thus, the IMF developed its World Economic Outlook review as the main vehicle for monitoring policy interactions and systemic developments.

In conducting World Economic Outlook discussions, country-specific analyses provide critical input, but their focus is global, centered on interdependence and aimed at appraising how appropriate the mix of national policies — particularly those of the larger members — is for the stability of the system at large. These discussions supplement the bilateral aspect of surveillance by adding a multilateral dimension in order to discern global trends and their causes. They are the main instruments of multilateral surveillance, but not the only ones. Additional global overseeing by the institution takes the form of examinations of specific aspects of the international scene and their linkages to country policies (eg. issues relating to capital flows, international policy coordination, foreign indebtedness, and international liquidity).

Improving Surveillance Measures

A number of avenues are now being considered in order to close potential gaps in the monitoring process which escape or transcend both bilateral and multilateral dimensions. Additionally, a need has developed for regional surveillance in view of the advances made toward economic integration in various parts of the world. This is most notably the case in Europe, where economies are in close interdependence and where constraints have been set on national economic policy-making by pathbreaking events such as the liberalization of capital flows among major members of the EMS, and the drive toward a single market in Western Europe as a whole. Such developments call for supplementation of the current bilateral and multilateral surveillance exercises with discussions on regional issues that have global implications.

Another avenue that suggests itself in buttressing surveillance in its bilateral, regional, and multilateral aspects calls for supplementing the country-specific perspective with a policy-specific or problem-specific approach. This would entail a cross-country analysis of policy issues that are of relevance to the international economy as a whole, yet which by and large reflects the national policy stance of its larger members. This analysis might also extend to the economic problems that affect particular groups of countries. By 1998, some progress has already been made in this regard by institutional studies of a general nature, covering subjects such as policy coordination and international debt issues.

In order to move in these various directions, certainly procedures that are simple in character and which offer a prospect of ready acceptance by the membership must be developed. Procedures that rely on the array of instruments already at the disposal of the IMF can help. For example, the final statements of consultation missions, which aim briefly at distilling the essence of the relevant policy issues discussed, could serve as the basis for the preparation of a summary policy paper on issues involving several members, and for discussion with appropriate officials representing those members. A brief report could then be prepared for the Executive Board's information or for discussion within the Board at large or, if necessary, within appropriate Executive Board Committees.

Two important benefits would derive from the introduction of procedures such as these. One would be to bring within the purview of the IMF membership issues of interest that are currently discussed within narrower forums, such as the Group of Five, the Group of Seven, and the Group of Ten. The procedures need not preclude these forums, but linking them to the IMF would strengthen the legitimacy of the surveillance process and of the institution itself. Another important advantage is that procedures involving full membership strengthen the rule of law and promote observance of the code of conduct.

In sum, surveillance involves policy discussions between the IMF and individual members as the basis for the formulation of an international community purview and the assessment of specific country policies. In addition, it encompasses regular examinations of the state of and prospects for the world economy as a whole, or of particular aspects of the international economic scene. The end purpose of these various activities is to promote consistency of national policies and aims to highlight interdependencies, and to point toward a well-balanced and fair assignment of policy responsibilities among members.

Taken from a broad vantage point, most of the other functions of the IMF are ultimately diverse modalities of surveillance. This fact does not deny their importance as distinct institutional responsibilities, but emphasizes the central unity that characterizes the fundamental identity of the IMF. In many respects, each of the functions of the institution is perceived as separate, and for certain purposes, such a separation is appropriate. It is important, however, to keep in mind their essentially unified character, as this is the IMF's particular distinction.

Financial Assistance and Conditionality

A large part of the IMF's function in maintaining international economic vibrancy is fulfilled by funding operations. The general rationale for the IMF's lending of financial support to members is characterized by Article I(v) of the Articles of Agreement:

> "To give confidence to members by making the general resources of the Fund temporarily available to them under adequate safeguards, thus providing them with the opportunity to correct maladjustments in their balance of payments without resorting to measures destructive of national or international prosperity."

Part of the Fund's traditional philosophy as regards this role has been that it was a credit cooperative whose resources were used on a 'revolving fund' basis. The financing programs that derived from such an approach aimed for quick results, and the institution was generally reluctant to accept a situation in which a country was making repeated use of its facilities. Over the last few decades, the Fund has come to recognize that effective support for countries deeply rooted in structural weaknesses require a much longer credit term. As a result, at least in the case of low-income nations, the Fund now only requires that 'substantial progress' should be the country's objective within the short-term period of three years. At the same time, the Fund has similarly moved toward a *de facto* acceptance of the repeated use of its credit facilities by developing country members, further diluting the original principle that it would only lend on a 'temporary' basis. Although it does not formally encourage more than three successive programs, the Board is willing to go along with prolonged use so long as this is carefully justified in the papers presented to it for adjudication. With these changes in disposition, financial assistance has taken on a more active role in IMF operations.

It should be noted that although the IMF is said to 'lend' money, the transactions that take place differ markedly from the traditional 'loan'. Rather than simply providing money, the Fund exchanges hard currency for a member country's soft currency. Therefore in all cases, except that of the ESAF (see below), members transact with the Fund by purchasing other members' currencies or SDRs with an equivalent amount of their own currencies. Charges are levied on these drawings and the IMF requires that members re-purchase their own currencies from the IMF over a specified time. IMF financing is subject to Executive Board approval and, in most cases, to the member's commitment to take steps to address the causes of its payments imbalance (see below).

IMF's Sources of Finance

The bulk of the IMF's resources are derived from its members' quota subscriptions. The IMF Articles of Agreement, however, authorize the institution to borrow if necessary to supplement those resources. The Fund usually borrows from official sources such as governments and central banks and the Bank for International Settlements, but it is also authorized to borrow from private sources.

Two schemes — the General Arrangements to Borrow (GAB) and the more recently approved New Arrangements to Borrow (NAB) — are in place for IMF borrowing. The GAB are lines of credit from

11 industrial countries or their central banks[1] that are available under specified circumstances at market-related rates of interest. The IMF also has an associated arrangement with Saudi Arabia under similar terms. GAB credit lines may be made available to the IMF to finance any exchange transaction of GAB participants with the IMF.

Stricter criteria are in place for non-participants: drawings must be in connection with an IMF-supported adjustment program, and the situation must be deemed to be one that could threaten the stability of the international monetary system.

The NAB is an expanded version of the GAB. Under the NAB, potentially 25 participant countries and institutions would stand ready to lend the IMF up to SDR34 billion. NAB credit lines may be drawn on for the benefit of all NAB-participating countries or for non-participants under circumstances similar to, but somewhat more flexible than, those under the GAB.

The Monetary Model

Before the IMF grants any kind of financial assistance to member countries with deficits in their balance of payments, it makes an analysis, both quantitatively and qualitatively, of the policy measures necessary to overcome the problems. Only then can it reach judgement on whether a country's policies will be sufficient to restore balance and, if they are not, to insist on a strengthened policy package as a condition for IMF credit. A monetary model has been designed for this purpose, through which the Fund is able to chart both the performance criteria for the release of successive amounts of financial assistance and the benchmarks that play a major role in the reviews of such arrangements.

---

[1]Belgium, Canada, Deutsche Bundesbank, France, Italy, Japan, The Netherlands, Sveriges Riksbank, Swiss National Bank, United Kingdom, and United States.

The model was designed to study the effects on both income formation and the balance of payments of the two most important exogenous variables (variables determined outside the model) operating on the economies of the great majority of countries in the early post-war period. These are the autonomous changes in exports and the creation of domestic bank credit; or, in monetary terms, foreign and domestic autonomous additions to a country's money supply. Handling the effects of these two variables required a model that explicitly recognized a demand-for-money function. The evidence from many countries suggested that the simplest form of such a function — namely, assuming that the demand for money is proportional to income — would be a reasonable approximation. As a second behavioral equation, the model contained a function of the demand for imports.

In its simplest form, the full model is:

(1) $\Delta MO = k \Delta Y$

The change in a country's money supply (ΔMO) is proportional to the change in its income (ΔY) by a factor k, which is the inverse of the velocity of circulation of money (Y/MO); thus, $k = MO/Y$.

(2) $M = mY$

The demand for imports (M) is a function of a country's income (Y), where m is the country's marginal propensity to import.

(3) $\Delta MO = \Delta R + \Delta D$

The change in the money supply (ΔMO) is by definition equal to the change in a country's foreign reserves (ΔR) plus the change in the domestic credit of the banking system (ΔD).

> (4) $\Delta R = X - M + K$
>
> The change in foreign reserves (DR) is by definition equal to exports (X) minus imports, plus net capital inflows of the nonbank sector (K).

The dynamic character of this model derives from the fact that it contains both income and the change in income. Running the model results in values for certain variables — such as income and change in foreign reserves — as weighted averages of the values for the current and past years of exports, capital inflows of the non-bank sector, and the change in domestic credit of the banking system.

It should be noted that the IMF model reflects assumptions from both the Keynesian and monetarist schools of thought. The dynamic nature of the model, in contrast to most of the academic monetary models of the balance of payments, yields not only the final equilibrium value of the endogenous variables but also the time path toward these values. It is essential to be able to derive these short-term effects if the model is to be used in analyzing current policy problems and finding their solutions.

The set of four equations in the model constitutes the logical core of the IMF's programming exercise, which is known as 'financial programming'. Since the early 1950s, it has been the centerpiece of the analysis leading to IMF conditionality — the set of policy actions that a borrowing country must take in order to have access to IMF credit.

Conditionality

When it provides financial support to a member country, the IMF must be sure the member is pursuing policies that will ameliorate or eliminate its external payments problem. In this regard, conditionality is the term that has been coined to refer to the IMF's policies regarding use of its financial resources. Article V, Section 3(a) prescribes that in setting conditions on the use of its resources, the Fund will seek to help members solve their balance of payments problems 'in a manner consistent with the provisions' of the Articles of Agreement.

The conditions which the IMF attaches to its credit facilities cannot constitute a standard remedy, as the reasons for balance of payments difficulties vary. Conditionality always aims at restoring domestic and external balance and price stability. The program design normally involves fiscal and monetary policy measures, exchange rate policy, public sector reform, trade liberalization, and financial sector and labor market reforms.

> However this does not mean that these conditions are imposed on an ad hoc basis. While the specifics and details of the programs may vary, they are all underpinned by a common approach. The Executive Board's guidelines on conditionality:
>
> - encourage members to adopt corrective measures at an early stage;
> - stress that the IMF pays due regards to members' domestic social and political objectives, as well as economic priorities and circumstances;
> - permit flexibility in determining the number and content of performance criteria;
> - emphasises that IMF arrangements are decisions of the IMF that set out, in consultation with members, the conditions for its financial assistance.

Conditionality, being a flexible concept, thus allows the incorporation of 'soft' considerations, external to econometric equations provided by the monetary model, into the final decision to provide financial assistance. Credit arrangements are thus kept versatile and dynamic in meeting with the growing objectives. Therefore, major policy understandings on matters such as structural adjustment, price and trade liberalization, deregulation of the labor market, and privatization — that cannot be conveniently reduced into econometric equations — can be accounted for by conditionality. For example, what was previously an analytically neutral variable, 'credit creation', was made more discerning with regard to the private sector (usually to be encouraged) and the government sector (usually to be discouraged). The IMF also moved toward advising on specific types of taxes (with some taxes judged more acceptable than others) and on various types of expenditure, endorsing social safety nets and education, and frowning upon military and other non-productive expenditures.

However, the IMF's adjustment programs are not a painless panacea for the economically emaciated, and are usually accompanied by severe costs. Expenditure cuts and economic reforms will always hit particular groups or industries making unproductive use of scarce resources. These programs are therefore often condemned, particularly if they seem to have disproportionate effects on the poorest population groups. In the light of all the criticism directed at the IMF programs, it should be borne in mind that countries often apply to the Fund at a late stage, when all other sources of finance have dried up. The situation is often already so serious that, with or without the Fund program, drastic action is unavoidable.

IMF Financial Support

A member can immediately withdraw from the IMF 25% of its quota that it paid in gold or a convertible currency. If this is insufficient for its needs, a member may request more money from the IMF and can generally borrow cumulatively three times what it paid as a quota subscription. In lending to a member more than the initial 25% of its quota, the IMF is guided by two principles. First, the pool of currencies at the IMF's disposal exists for the benefit of the entire membership. Second, before the IMF releases any money from the pool, the member must demonstrate how it intends to solve its payments problem so that it can repay the Fund within its normal repayment period. An outline of the IMF's financial policies is provided below:

Reserve Tranche. A member has a reserve tranche position in the IMF to the extent that its quota exceeds the IMF's holding of its currency, excluding credits extended to it by the IMF. A member may draw up to the full amount of its reserve tranche position at any time, subject only to its balance of payments needs. This drawing does not constitute a use of IMF credit and is not subject to an obligation to repay.

Credit Tranche. Credits under regular facilities are made available to members in tranches or segments of 25% of the quota. For first credit tranche drawings, members are required to demonstrate reasonable efforts to overcome their balance of payments difficulties, and no phasing applies. Upper credit tranche drawings (over 25%) are normally phased in relation to performance criteria — such as budgetary and credit ceilings.

Policy on Emergency Assistance. The IMF provides emergency assistance, allowing members to make drawings to meet balance of payments needs arising from sudden and unforeseeable natural disasters and post-conflict situations. Such assistance can be extended in the form of outright purchases normally up to 25% of the quota, provided that the member is cooperating with the IMF. It does not entail performance criteria or a phasing of disbursements.

Debt and Debt-Service Reduction Policies. Part of the credit extended by the IMF to a member under regular facilities can be set aside to finance operations involving debt principal and debt service reduction. The exact amount set aside is determined on a case-by-case basis and its availability is generally phased in line with program performance.

Financial Facilities

Pursuant to its financial policies, the IMF has designed a variety of financial facilities to address specific problems. In the early 1980s, criticisms were mounted against the Fund for the inappropriateness of its funding packages with regard to the plight of developing nations. As a result, the IMF broadened the range of its financial mechanisms to include some that are sensitive to a wider variety of circumstances and problems.

Three broad groups of IMF financial facilities may be identified:

1. Regular IMF facilities

Stand-By Arrangements (SBA). This scheme is designed to provide short-term balance of payments assistance for deficits of a temporary or cyclical nature, and such arrangements are typically for 12 to 18 months. Drawings are phased on a quarterly basis, and their release is conditional upon meeting performance criteria and the completion of periodic program reviews. Performance criteria generally cover bank credit, government or public sector borrowing, trade and payments restrictions, foreign borrowing, and international reserve levels. Repurchases are made three to five years after each purchase.

Extended Fund Facility (EFF). The EFF is designed to support medium-term programs that generally run for three years. The EFF aims at overcoming balance of payments difficulties stemming from macro-economic and structural problems. Performance criteria are applied, similar to those in SBA, and repurchases are made in four to ten years.

2. Special facilities

Under this umbrella is the *Systemic Transformation Facility* (STF), which is a temporary facility designed to extend financial assistance to transition economies experiencing severe disruption in their trade and payments arrangements (repurchases are made over four to ten years). The second subset is the *Compensatory and Contingency Financing Facility* (CCFF) which provides financial assistance to countries experiencing temporary export shortfalls, and compensatory financing for excesses in cereal import costs, as well as for external contingencies in Fund arrangements (repurchases are made over three to five years). The CCFF is usually used in conjunction with other facilities such as the SBA.

3. Concessional IMF facilities

Structural Adjustment Facility (SAF). When it became clear that the least developed members of the IMF could not cope with their debt problems in the framework of the usual strict modalities of IMF credit arrangements, a special facility was developed which stood apart from the monetary character of the Fund. This facility — the Structural Adjustment Facility — has been available to the poorest countries since 1986. The facility provides funds for economic reform programs on favorable terms — a low interest rate of 0.5% and long term repayment of up to ten years. This facility was extended to become the ESAF.

Enhanced Structural Adjustment Facility (ESAF). Established in 1987 and extended in 1994, the ESAF is designed for low-income member countries with protracted balance of payments problems. ESAF drawings are loans and not purchases of other members' currencies. The facility is financed by a large group of countries, many of them emerging market economies and former beneficiaries of the program.

ESAF resources are intended to support strong medium-term structural adjustment programs. Under the facility, eligible members must develop — with the assistance of the staff from the IMF and the World Bank — a policy framework paper (PFP) for a three-year adjustment program. The PFP, which is updated annually, describes the authorities' economic objectives, macroeconomic and structural policies, and associated external financing needs and major sources of financing.

ESAF credit bears an annual interest rate of 0.5%, with a five-year grace period and a ten-year maturity. Quarterly benchmarks and semi-annual performance criteria apply. By common consent, performance and monitoring provisions are much more stringent for ESAF credits, since the intention of the scheme is that it should only be linked to especially vigorous policy reforms.

Objectives of Financial Support

The above discussion of the schematics behind IMF funding must be understood in the light of the objectives that underlie the function.

The Fund has long described the objective of its financial assistance function as the restoration of viability to the borrowing country's balance of payments. Traditionally, the view is that the IMF's primary role is in strengthening a country's payments position and that, by doing so, it was laying the foundation upon which improved growth could be achieved for the future. This position directs the focus of the IMF on balance of payments issues and relegates growth as a subsidiary concern. However, with changes in the understanding of the global economic climate, there has been mounting pressure from the international community for the IMF to be more directly active in areas of growth. By 1990, the language used to describe the objective of financial assistance began to be couched in these terms. In the case of ESAF programs, the objective has been formally redefined so as to elevate economic growth as a primary objective.

The IMF has also responded to the urgings of UNICEF and other organizations towards giving its programs more of a 'human face'. The traditional Fund position was that it was a matter for the respective governments to concern themselves with the distributional impact of stabilization programs, and that it would be inappropriate for the Fund to get involved in such matters. This position has gradually changed. Fund missions now commonly discuss distributional aspects with governments when preparing programs, and there is a requirement that the Policy Framework Papers prepared in connection with ESAF programs should 'identify measures that can help cushion the possible adverse effects of certain policies on vulnerable groups in ways consistent with the program's macroeconomic framework'.[2]

Interestingly, environmental concerns have also surfaced as an issue in funding policies. However, despite strong efforts from the environmentalist lobby, the US Administration, the European representatives at the Board and some other shareholders, have been quite dismissive of the relevance of environmental issues to IMF operations, and even view them as concessions that might dilute the macroeconomic functions of the institution. A tentative compromise has been reached whereby a resolution was made that the IMF 'should be mindful of the interplay between economic policies, economic activity, and environmental change, and that it should avoid policies that could have undesirable environmental consequences in ways consistent with the Fund's mandate, size, and structure'.[3]

---

[2] IMF, *Annual Report 1991*: 51-2.
[3] IMF, *Annual Report 1991*: 54.

Identity Crisis:
The IMF in the 1970s

After a decade of expanding international trade under a regime of stable exchange rates, the international monetary system — with the IMF as its stalwart — was about to face its biggest challenge. The dramatic economic developments that erupted in the 1970s presented problems that exceeded in magnitude and complexity anything the world had seen since the Great Depression of the 1930s. The international monetary system of adjustable pegs anchored to American dollars, adopted at Bretton Woods, collapsed when America decided to suspend convertibility of their currency into gold. The system (or non-system) which replaced it was confronted with the problem of determining new monetary parities and their margin of fluctuations.

What Happened?

From as early as the 1950s, the system of par value showed signs of increasing strain. This was largely due to a reversal of competitive positions between the major industrial countries. War-torn Europe (especially Germany) and Japan emerged as new economic powers, while the United States was beginning to undergo more rapid inflation and was persistently dogged by a balance of payments deficit. When the United States attempted to deal with its domestic unemployment

Identity Crisis: The IMF in the 1970s

in the 1960s by expanding its monetary base, this caused inflation which meant that the dollar was effectively overvalued. However, the United States was unable to devalue its currency under the Bretton Woods system. Under such a system whereby overvalued or undervalued currencies could not adjust themselves because of their commitments to par values, an environment conducive to speculative attacks emerged.

In 1968, the British balance of payments deficit led the speculators to conclude that devaluation was imminent despite a loan made available by the IMF. A massive attack was launched against the sterling pound, and it collapsed after the Central Bank of England mopped up over £1 billion. This was followed by the devaluation of the French franc in May in the same year. Similarly, the United States was suffering from persistent trade deficits which ballooned to $10 billion by 1970. These deficits naturally implied that there were matching surpluses elsewhere, notably Germany. Given the fixed exchange rates, German Marks began to look seriously undervalued against the dollar. Speculators exploited the inconsistency and applied upward pressure on the Mark by buying it. Obliged to maintain the exchange rate of $0.27 to the Mark, the Germans acquired billions in international reserves, thereby expanding their monetary base. As this would have a strong inflationary impact on the economy, the Bundesbank decided to allow the Mark to float and it appreciated by 3.7%.

The persistent balance of payments deficits of the US gave rise to the sentiment that the dollar was overvalued. This perception was strengthened by the high inflation rate in the US. Because of the unpopularity of the war in Vietnam, the US government was unable to increase taxation to finance its military efforts in Vietnam. As a result, excessive money was created instead to support the war. Contributing much to the deficit was also the huge capital outflows into Europe as direct investments.

As the United States financed its deficits with dollars, dollar holdings grew and consequently so did potential claims on US gold reserves. Under the Bretton Woods system, the United States acted as the 'world's banker', because the US dollar was used as an international currency. As such, the United States was able to meet its balance of payments by issuing more dollars. The rest of the industrialized powers began to feel that America was abusing its position by running persistent balance of payments deficits, and flushing the world with excessive liquidity.

As the US deficits persisted and increased over time, foreign-held reserves exceeded US gold reserves. The refusal of Germany and Japan to re-value ultimately forced the United States to devalue its currency. In August 1971, President Nixon announced his decision to end the convertibility of the US dollar to gold as part of his 'new economic policy'.

While it was the United States' large balance of payments deficits that ultimately triggered the collapse of the Bretton Woods system, other profound economic problems — international liquidity and the lack of adjustment flexibility — eventually lead to a loss of confidence that wrecked the international monetary system in the 1970s.

International liquidity is vital for nations to be able to finance temporary balance of payments deficits without resorting to trade restrictions, while at the same time adjustment mechanisms are allowed to operate so that the deficit will eventually be corrected. Hence insufficient liquidity would curtail the growth of global trade. However, excessive liquidity would lead to worldwide inflationary pressures. Under the Bretton Woods system, most of the world's liquidity was created out of the US' financing of its balance of payments deficits. The longer these deficits remained unresolved, the more unwanted dollars were being held in foreign hands, leading eventually to a loss of confidence in the dollar. (Ironically, when the US was running trade surpluses the international monetary system was threatened with illiquidity, and the dollar shortage of the 1950s and early 1960s became the dollar glut of the late 1960s.)

Identity Crisis: The IMF in the 1970s

Saving the System

The global economy was suddenly faced with the prospect of having no common exchange rate system; no clearly defined set of rules for official intervention; no effective control over the growth of international liquidity; and no clearly specified obligations with respect to balance of payments adjustments. Above all, there were no clearly defined rights and obligations of governments in their international monetary relations. In short, after the collapse of Bretton Woods there was no clear 'monetary system', and representatives from the Group of Ten nations met at the Smithsonian Institution in Washington in 1971, in an attempt to re-establish the adjustable peg.

They tried to set new parities for the major currencies of the world, drew a 9% band around the new rates for fluctuations, and set a new price for gold at $38 an ounce. The agreement reached became known as the Smithsonian Agreement, but it did not succeed in solving the problems caused by the dollar's abrupt inconvertibility.

These alterations were, however, unacceptable to some European countries, and instead they decided to let their currencies float jointly against the dollar with a total band of fluctuation of 2.25%. The Smithsonian variation was said to provide the framework or tunnel within which the smaller Europe currencies moved. Hence this partial break became commonly known as the 'European snake' or the 'snake in the tunnel'.

At the same time, outlines for a new international monetary system to replace the defunct par value was also being worked out by a group of IMF staff known as the Committee of Twenty. Like the Group of Ten, the committee attempted to re-establish a structure which aimed to be as stable as that previously devised at Bretton Woods, and at the same time introduce a more satisfactory adjustment mechanism and greater control over the growth of international liquidity. However, it soon emerged that this was too enormous a task, and details of a precisely crafted system seemed increasingly impossible to reach. Likewise, the Smithsonian agreement ended in failure.

The Committee of Twenty eventually abandoned its attempt to overhaul the international monetary system and adopted the more modest objective of trying to formulate principles that would guide members in the conduct of their exchange rate policies. In the early days of the new managed float system, there was great anxiety of returning to the days of competitive devaluation of the 1930s. This, however, did not materialize.

A New Era

The breakdown of the old system under the auspices of the IMF led some commentators to conclude that the IMF had lost its *raison d'être*, and that its continued function and influence over the monetary system should cease. However the IMF was quick to re-invent itself, and it could be said that the absence of any clear system all the more accentuated the need for some form of international regulatory body. This was a void which the IMF, given its history and experience, was ready and eager to fill. As a result of the evolution of the whole system of international payments, the IMF had to modify its Articles of Agreement, which it did in Jamaica in 1976.

The Jamaica Agreement altered the articles of the IMF firstly by legalizing the floating exchange rate system, which was paramount. Secondly, it was also decided that the IMF would watch over exchange rates agreements, increase the quotas of member states, and establish a fund to assist the underdeveloped countries.

The new Articles of Agreement of 1978 formally provide that members can adopt the exchange arrangements of their choice. However, this new freedom is not entirely unfettered, as firm surveillance by the IMF will be exercised under specific principles adopted for the guidance of all members. In contrast to the Bretton Woods order — under which exchange rates had been subject to agreed rules — the exchange rates of a member became a variable within the arsenal of domestic economic policies. Concomitantly, the function of the IMF shifted from that of policing member states' commitment to an agreed rate of exchange to that of overseeing a specific country's exchange rate policy.

Not only was this sanctioned system very different from the original Bretton Woods system, but the free and non-discriminatory trade philosophy which has been given the accolade of rebuilding Europe after WWII was now under threat. Protectionism re-emerged as a significant issue in world trade, especially when developing countries increasingly tried to solve their own economic growth, unemployment, and external debt problems by rapidly expanding their exports to the industrialized countries.

Further Economic Turbulence in the 1970s

The 1970s started off on the wrong foot. Many of the main industrialized countries were plagued by a slump that began in 1969. Adding to the problem, the oil crisis of 1973 and the excessively deflationary policies that the industrialized countries adopted in response, led (in 1973–75) to the deepest international recession in four decades. Despite the simulative policies in several industrialized countries, the pace of subsequent recovery was so slow that it depressed the levels of employment and the volume of world trade.

The preceding period of lightning growth in the 1950s and 1960s was put in doubt as an anomaly rather than the result of sound policies and as 'natural' economic development. Part of the slowdown can be explained on the basis of more costly raw materials and energy, which was in abundance in the earlier decades. In 1972, the Club of Rome warned of the shortages of natural resources and that the risks of air and water pollution could seriously cap economic growth. This anticipated crisis was felt most acutely in 1973, after scarce supplies of oil led to a sharp appreciation of prices.

This period also saw the novel occurrence of stagflation (a combination of high unemployment and inflation) which proved to be a costly problem for traditional macroeconomic thought and policies, since contractionary fiscal and monetary policies for containing inflation would heighten the problem of unemployment, whereas expansionary policies for boosting the economy and reducing unemployment would only accentuate inflationary pressures.

As a result of the Yom Kipper War of 1973, oil supplies were effectively cut off. When they resumed with inadequate supplies, prices rose by 400%. It is estimated that this cost the oil-importing countries an extra $100 billion per year. Since the introduction of floating rates the US dollar has suffered significant devaluation. The decline of the dollar proved to be a decisive development, since it was used to quote oil prices. The price hike imposed by OPEC therefore found its justification here. The sudden quadrupling of the prices for crude oil came as a shock to the world, and costs of production were commensurately raised in industrialized and developing countries, further aggravating inflation. The fear of limited raw resources was further inflamed by episodic crop failures in 1972 and 1973. This led to speculative rushes into commodities which were to characterize the rest of the decade, and which also pushed up the prices of primary products. Prices of grains and of cotton, wool, rubber and most metals soared to unprecedented levels.

The onset of the oil crisis had protracted ramifications. For one, oil-importing developing countries were left with an onerous legacy of debt which they have been living with ever since. The huge balance of payments deficits and external debt accrued as a result of the price hike also lowered the credit ratings of these economies, making it more difficult for them to obtain financial assistance.

A New Agenda for the IMF

The combination of high rates of inflation and the excessively steep increases in oil prices caused massive balance of payments deficits for the oil-importing countries, and many of the IMF's member states

Identity Crisis: The IMF in the 1970s

faced a severe worldwide recession. After the first oil crisis, the Fund opened a credit facility in 1974 and 1975 for countries affected by the sharp increase in oil prices. Under this Oil Facility (OF), the IMF borrowed funds from the petroleum-exporting nations to lend to the deficit nations at competitive rates. By 1976, it had already used a total of 6.9 billion SDRs. As payments deficits persisted, the Fund continued to seek new arrangements for financing these deficits. Thus, the period saw the proliferation of IMF facilities and a shift in focus toward a greater involvement in developing countries despite the breakdown of the Bretton Woods order. The introduction of the Extended Fund Facility (for adjustment programs of medium-term duration) and the supplementary financing facility enabled the Fund to lend larger multiples of quotas.

As another measure to combat the oil price hike, a subsidy account to reduce the cost of drawings under the 1975 oil facility by lower income developing members was implemented. The Fund also liberalized and extended its compensatory financing facility, expanded the applications for the buffer stock facility, and established a trust fund for its poorest members, financed by the proceeds from the sale of one-sixth of the Fund's gold.

As can be seen, given the economic turbulence of the 1970s, the Fund's lending activities became a more pronounced feature. A significant development in this direction was its ability to extend loans above and beyond a country's contribution in the form of quotas to the Fund under its supplementary financing facilities. Increasingly, the Fund began to act as a financial intermediary, borrowing from its more affluent members to lend to their poverty-stricken counterparts.

The 1980s: The Debt Crisis

The 1980s marked a major transition in the balance of payments accounts for many developing countries. Third World nations operated with sizeable current account deficits as imports of capital and intermediate goods were required to provide the machinery and equipment for rapid industrialization. Export earnings paid for most, but not all of these imports.

These deficits were mainly financed by large resource transfers in the form of country-to-country (bilateral) foreign aid, direct private investment by multinational corporations, private loans by international banks, and multilateral loans from the World Bank and other international development agencies. By borrowing heavily abroad, developing countries continued to grow at a relatively rapid pace even during the second half of the 1970s. However, in the early 1980s, their huge and fast-expanding foreign debts caught up with them and large-scale defaults were averted by official intervention by the IMF.

Before the 1970s, the external debts of developing countries were relatively small and primarily an official phenomenon, meaning that the majority of creditors were foreign governments and international financial institutions such as the World Bank, the IMF, and regional development banks. Most loans were on low-interest terms and were

The 1980s: The Debt Crisis

extended for purposes of implementing development projects and expanding imports of capital goods. However, while foreign borrowing can be highly beneficial and provides the resources to promote economic development, it is also very costly. More significantly, an increasing portion of the debt was now on non-concessional terms involving shorter maturities and market rates of interest.

During the early 1980s, commercial banks began playing a larger role in international lending by recycling surplus OPEC 'petrodollars' and issuing general-purpose loans to less developed countries to provide balance of payments support and aid the expansion of export sectors. Although many developing countries intended to use the money to improve standards of living, little of the borrowed money benefited the poor in the end. Across the board, about a fifth went to arms, often to shore up oppressive regimes. Further, many governments initiated poorly planned large-scale development projects, many of which proved to be completely useless. And all too often money was siphoned off into private bank accounts.

In the mid-1970s, many Third World countries adopted an export-led growth strategy. They specialized in producing cash crops such as coffee, tea, cocoa and cotton. However, far too many of them were producing the same raw materials, and as a result prices tumbled. The second oil shock, which occurred in 1979, brought about a complete reversal of the economic conditions conducive to the success of international lending in the previous period. Developing countries now faced an abrupt increase in oil prices that added to oil import bills and affected industrial goods imports. There was also a huge interest rate increase caused by the industrialized countries' economic stabilization policies and a decrease in Third World export earnings, resulting from a combination of slowed growth in the more developed nations and a precipitous decline of over 20% in primary commodity export prices. In addition, developing nations inherited from the previous periods a huge debt and debt-service obligation, which was made even more oppressive by burgeoning interest rates and more precarious as a result of the bunching of short-term maturities.

Finally, during the entire period of debt accumulation, one of the most significant and persistent trends was the tremendous increase in private capital flight. Between 1976 and 1985, it is estimated that about $200 billion fled the heavily indebted countries. This was coupled with an increasing external debt that doubled from $68.4 billion to $1,283 billion between 1970 to 1989.

Faced with this critical situation, Third World countries had two options. They could both curtail imports and impose restrictive fiscal and monetary measures, thus impeding growth and development objectives, or they could finance their widening current account deficits through further external borrowing. Unable and sometimes reluctant to adopt the first option as a means of solving the balance of payments crisis, many countries were forced in the early 1980s to rely on the second option, borrowing even more heavily. As a result, massive debts and debt-service obligations accumulated, so that by the middle 1980s, countries like Brazil, Mexico, Argentina, the Philippines and Chile faced severe difficulties in paying even the interest on their debts from export earnings.

Nor could these countries borrow funds from the private capital markets any longer. In fact, not only did private lending dry up, but by 1986, the developing countries were paying back $11.3 billion more to the commercial banks than they were receiving in new loans. Facing default, many developing countries were forced to renegotiate their debt repayment schedules and interest payments with their creditor banks in the developed countries, with the help of the IMF and under its general direction. As part of the deal, austerity measures were finally imposed to reduce imports and to cut inflation, wages and other social expenditure, so as to put domestic growth on a more sustainable basis. Now these highly indebted countries had no choice but to seek the IMF's aid and accept the conditions under which the aid would be offered.

Some of these conditions included:

- Abolition or liberalization of foreign exchange and import controls.
- Devaluation of the official exchange rate.
- A stringent domestic, anti-inflation program consisting of a) control of bank credit to raise interest rates and reserve requirements; b) control of government deficit through curbs on spending, especially in the areas of social services for the poor and staple food subsidies, along with increases in taxes and in public enterprise prices; c) control of wage increases, in particular assuring that such increases are at rates less than the inflation rate (in effect abolishing wage indexing); and d) dismantling of various forms of price controls.
- Greater hospitality to foreign investment and a general opening up of the economy to international commerce.

While such conditions may have been successful in improving the debt-ridden countries' balance of payments situation, they could politically be very unpopular because they strike at the heart of development efforts by unevenly hurting the lower- and middle-income groups.

Alternatively, they have been viewed by Third World countries as a double standard — harsh adjustment policies for the LDC debtors and no adjustment of the huge budget and/or trade deficits for the world's greatest debtor — the United States. However, the prospect of growth coming to a grinding halt led the indebted countries of Latin America to reject the austerity plans put forward by the IMF. It was under such circumstances that the Baker Plan was proposed in 1985.

The Baker Plan

Named after US Treasury Secretary, James Baker, this plan was based on the premise that 'sustainable growth with adjustment must be the central objective of the debt strategy' and emphasized growth over austerity. It also postulated that there should be a greater flow of capital from developed nations and the World Bank. However, the large commercial banks were reluctant to lend their support to this scheme, preferring to write off some of their bad loans and sell others on the secondary market at a heavy discount. Thus, the Baker Plan failed to make any substantial improvement and the debt problem persisted.

In 1986, the IMF established the Structural Adjustment Facility (described in Chapter 5) to provide balance of payments assistance on concessional terms to the least developed member nations which could not cope with their debt problems in the framework of the usual strict modalities of IMF credit arrangements. Although the structural adjustment facilities were intended to expire, the IMF decided to continue the ESAF and even further extend it. The SAF/ESAF programs have proved very successful in helping many developed countries pursue an appropriate macroeconomic policy.

To provide further relief for the debt crisis, in the same year, on 3–4 April, the Interim Committee asked the Executive Board to consider proposals by US Treasury Secretary, Nicholas F. Brady.

The Brady Plan

In 1989, debts to commercial banks were no longer worth their value on paper because the banks had in theory written off large chunks of them, assuming they would never be repaid. Brady argued that the banks should reduce the actual value of the remaining debts for larger debtor countries so that they had less to pay.

The banks would do this in one of two ways. The first was to write off some of the debts with the help of funds from the IMF and the World Bank. The second way was to reschedule some of the remaining debts by converting them to bonds and selling them on the secondary market. For this purpose, the IMF could set aside, for debt reduction purposes, 25% of the resources normally available under a Fund program. Additional aid could also be granted for interest payments up to a maximum of 40% of the quota. Mexico was the first to sign the agreement.

This plan achieved better results than the Baker Plan and many countries gained access to the international capital markets. As a result, the severity of the debt program moderated considerably in Latin America.

Payment Arrears

During the debt crisis, the IMF discovered that it was being confronted by late payments in the repayment of loans. It became clear that the IMF, perhaps as a result of the criticism regarding conditionality or due to political pressure, had awarded some countries loans far exceeding their ability to repay them.

Thus the arrears which Sudan alone owes the IMF are already far more than one year of its export earnings. This was not in accordance with the IMF's task of making available, temporary, revolving resources. But even the repayments of countries which do meet their obligations are very high in relation to their economic performance.

The IMF has made various attempts to solve the arrears problem, but has not been very successful. The number of countries with long-term arrears has declined somewhat, but those that remain appear to be entrenched in this problem. The amount of arrears has risen to nearly SDR3 billion in 1995. Countries that fail to erase these debts even after repeated pressure are soon excluded from further use of Fund resources. Since 1985, 11 countries have received a declaration of 'ineligibility to use the Fund's resources', six of which have since paid off their debts.

As all nations should bear the burden of the global debt crisis, the IMF established special reserves, the Special Contingency Accounts, in view of the growing arrears. These reserves were funded by surcharges on the Fund's interest revenue from debtor countries that do pay, and reductions in the interest paid by the Fund to creditor countries.

This burden sharing also protects the IMF from the loss of interest revenue sharing resulting from the arrears. Together with the general reserves, these precautionary balances now total around 10% of the total outstanding credit. The optimal level of such precautionary balances to cover the risks the Fund incurs should also be based on the degree of concentration of Fund exposure in certain large countries, such as Mexico and Russia, but always contains a subjective element. For the Fund to remain a financially solid institution, it is imperative that a sufficiently strong buffer is maintained. Owing to its unique financial structure, it is nonetheless acceptable that the ratio of precautionary balances to credit is somewhat lower than that for the World Bank (presently over 15%), which seeks to maintain the confidence of the international capital markets.

In the case of countries which are ready to find a solution, the IMF responds by setting up support groups of friendly industrialized donor countries, which provide financial support for a shadow program. With the aid of such a program, which resembles an IMF program but without the loan of the IMF itself, an effort is made to restore the country's creditworthiness and to enable it to pay off its arrears to the IMF. For some countries such as Guyana, Somalia and Vietnam, support groups are active, with Canada, Italy and France respectively playing a pioneering role for these countries.

In 1990, the IMF decided to take tougher action by depriving countries with long-term arrears of their right to vote in the Fund. This proposal from the US was accepted by other countries with some reluctance since it necessitated amending the Articles of Agreement — a rather cumbersome procedure generally reserved for more fundamental matters. Nevertheless, there was little choice as the United States linked its proposal to its approval of the ninth quota increase, where it was able to form a blocking minority.

For some poor developing countries, the debt to multilateral institutions remains particularly high. For 12 countries, among them Guyana, Mozambique, Nicaragua, Tanzania and Uganda, even if 90%

of their non-multilateral debts were forgiven, their remaining debt ratio would be at an unsustainable level of over 200% of the value of annual exports of goods and services.

References

1. Bakker, A.F.P., *International Financial Institutions*, 1996, 1st ed., Longman, UK.
2. Todaro, Michael P., *Economic Development in the Third World*, 1992, 4th ed., Longman, UK.
3. Drisco, David D., *What is the International Monetary Fund?*, 1997, 1st ed., International Monetary Fund, Washington, D.C.
4. Salvatore, Dominick, *International Trade Policy*, 1993, 1st ed., Macmillan Publishing Company, New York.
5. Guitian, Manuel, *The Unique Nature of the Responsibilities of the International Monetary Fund*, 1992, 1st ed., International Monetary Fund, Washington, D.C.

Recent Efforts: The HIPC Initiative

In October 1996, there was a major shift by the IMF and the World Bank when they produced a debt relief initiative which contemplated for the first time the cancellation of the debts owed to them. The agreement also recommended a strategy to enable countries to exit from unsustainable debt burdens. Britain's chancellor proposed that the initiative should be financed through the sale of IMF gold. The initiative proposed 80% debt relief by the key creditor countries (Japan, US, Germany, France and UK).

The central aim of the initiative was to enable highly indebted poor countries to achieve a sustainable debt level within a period of six years and thus an exit from the rescheduling process. During the six-year period, a country has to implement a World Bank/IMF-supported adjustment program. The first three-year stage is based on current debt relief mechanisms. At the decision point which marks the end of the first stage, the Paris Club creditors will provide eligible countries with stock-of-relief under Naples terms (67% reduction on the eligible debt stock). Other bilateral and commercial creditors are to provide comparable treatment, while the multilaterals continue to provide adjustment support.

If these actions do not result in a sustainable debt level, a country goes on to the second stage of the initiative. During this stage, bilateral and commercial debt service reduction, in Net Present Value (NPV) terms, is topped up to 80%. The World Bank may also provide enhanced support in the form of IDA grants during this interim period. At the completion point which marks the end of the second stage, the country will, if necessary, receive 80% bilateral and commercial debt stock reduction, provided that its adjustment track record is still sound. Should this still not prove sufficient, the multilateral creditors will provide debt relief to the point where the country's debt will be reduced to a sustainable level.

The total cost of the initiative over an eight-year period for the 41 countries classified as the heavily indebted poor countries (HIPCs) is estimated at around US$5 billion. The multilateral creditors have established a HIPC Trust Fund, which will act as the instrument with which relief on the debt they are owed is provided. Bilateral contributions will be important to facilitate full participation of all multilateral creditors.

One of the major vehicles within the HIPC initiative is the Debt Sustainability Analysis (DSA). The purpose of this DSA is to assess whether a country is able to meet its current and future external obligations in full without compromising economic growth and without resorting to rescheduling or building up arrears in the future. The debt sustainability targets under the initiative are to be set within the range of 200-250% for the NPV debt-to-exports ratio and 20–25% for the debt service ratio. On the basis of a vulnerability analysis, it is to be decided if the country's targets should be set to the lower or upper limits of the range. The DSA is of crucial importance to the final determination of the amount of debt relief necessary for a country to achieve a sustainable level of debt and an exit from the debt rescheduling process.

Criticism

Recently there has been real concern that the HIPC initiative will join the long list of failed efforts to solve the debt crisis in the Third World.

One of the main weaknesses highlighted is that it takes far too long to release the required funds which the scheme promises. So far only six countries have entered the HIPC out of which only three — Uganda, Bolivia and Guyana — will receive the debt relief by 1998. Mozambique, Burkina Faso and Ivory Coast will not benefit until 1999, 2000 and 2001 respectively.

This delay is largely due to the strict interpretations of the HIPC rules which demand compliance with IMF reform programs. Non-governmental organizations, particularly Oxfam, have argued that the rules have to take into greater consideration these countries' crippling poverty and that the amount of debt repayment required will severely hamper social spending on health and education.

IMF and the Crisis

The intention of this chapter is not to chronicle the already well-documented Asian economic crisis nor to set out to examine the causes of the crisis, which would require a book in itself. The purpose here is to highlight its main features and characteristics so as to provide a context in which we view the IMF's response to it. Specifically, this chapter will attempt to capture the sudden loss of confidence in the 'tiger' economies, which became a key problem when the IMF was initially attempting to tackle by raising interest rates and imposing austerity measures.

The Asian crisis occurred against a backdrop of years of breathtaking growth. A hallmark of this success was the unprecedented vast inflows of foreign capital in the 1990s. At their height, net private capital inflows constituted as much as 13% of Thailand's GDP and 17% of Malaysia's. With Japan and Europe experiencing weak growth since the early 1990s, despite the low interest rates, domestic investment was well below available savings. Emerging markets seemed like an irresistible catch. Large private capital flows were driven to a large extent by this over-zealous search for high yields without proper regard to potential pitfalls. To some extent this optimism concerning the Asian economies and the rapid growth they were experiencing masked much of those economies' weaknesses. The crisis, therefore, in more concrete terms, was the reversal of this tide of capital flow.

Many of the economies in the region were overheating, as was evidenced by the large and persistent current account deficits and the property and stock market bubbles. Their current account deficits, on average, hovered around a risky 5% of their respective GDP range. Lawrence Summers warned in an article in *The Economist* after the Mexican crisis that a deficit above 5% of a country's GDP is of particular concern and poses questions of sustainability, especially when it is financed in such a way that could lead to rapid capital reversals.

While the deficits were not the result of either extravagant governmental expenditure or excessive private consumption, but rather due to high levels of investment, investors were getting increasingly suspicious of the quality and nature of these investments. It seemed that the huge amounts of money pouring into the non-tradable sector was ill-advised for two reasons. Firstly, it contributed to a property and stock market bubble, and secondly, investment in property does not translate into the production of exportable goods, which could then be sold to finance the current account deficit. In addition, investments in other sectors were simply unprofitable — the return on the investment exceeded the cost of borrowing. To a large extent, this influenced the IMF to implement austerity programs in order to address the problem of current account imbalances.

The maintenance of pegged exchange rates went on for too long, leading to several adverse effects on many of the ASEAN countries that had fixed their currencies to the US dollar. For one, it vitiated their export competitiveness as it strengthened against the other major currencies as a result of the appreciation of the dollar. The situation was not helped by a general slump in the electronics sector, in which a number of the ASEAN economies were heavily engaged. And finally, export prospects were further impaired by the Chinese devaluation of the yuan. Collectively, these factors gave rise to doubts regarding the sustainability of their current account deficits.

Furthermore, the pegged exchanged rate distorted the risk of borrowing, encouraged inordinate external borrowing and led to a high incidence of exposure to foreign exchange risk in both the financial and corporate sectors. This imprudence was exacerbated by lax banking rules and gross financial oversight. The high incidence of bankruptcies before the crisis and the significant proportion of non-performing loans amongst the banks in the region were testimony of a poorly-regulated financial sector and of perverse links between banks and companies. As a result, financial and banking sector reforms are the main features of the IMF-led programs

As the crisis unfolded, political uncertainties and doubts about the governments' commitment to and competence in rectifying the situation by implementing painful but requisite measures and reforms dragged the currencies and stock markets down to new depths. Manifest reluctance to tighten monetary conditions and to wind up insolvent financial institutions raised doubts about the governments' ability to restore confidence and stability in their economies.

The first domino to fall was Thailand, where the currency had been under episodic speculative attacks since the beginning of 1996. The baht came under renewed downward pressure in the first two months of 1997, as concerns intensified regarding the sustainability of the peg to the US dollar in the face of persistent current account deficits; an onerously high short-term external debt; the collapse of an asset price bubble; and the loss of external competitiveness as the dollar strengthened against the Japanese yen. To fend off the attacks on the baht, the authorities intervened in the spot and forward exchange markets and forced the interest rates up to diminish capital outflow. However, the measures were regarded as being a case of too little, too late, especially in terms of their lack of action in tackling the more fundamental problems of weakness in the financial sector.

Severe pressures re-emerged in early May, prompting the central bank to introduce more extreme measures of direct capital and exchange controls, adding to its earlier repertoire of intervening in the spot and forward exchange markets and in maintaining high interest rates. Again these measures failed to soothe the strains on the Thai currency and confidence in the economy was further undermined. This was partly due to a situation beyond the domestic control of the Thai authorities. A tightening in global financial conditions had resulted after the sudden rise in Japanese bond yields and the sharp rebound in the yen, which reduced the attraction of borrowing from Japan to finance investment in markets elsewhere. This caused particular problems for some emerging economies in the region that had grown accustomed to short-term capital inflows. Hence investors, local and foreign alike, took on short positions against the baht, which they concluded was a safe bet given the exchange rate peg, weak fundamentals and relatively low funding costs.

In the face of a sustained challenge against the baht, the Thais decided on the fateful July 2nd to abandon its peg exchange rate against the dollar and allowed the currency to float. After dropping initially by approximately 10%, the baht continued to weaken in subsequent weeks as concerns intensified about both the uncertain political situation and the delay in the adoption of a comprehensive economic package to support the new exchange rate regime and to deal with the frail financial system. News of the fact that the authorities almost emptied their reserves in defending the baht did not bode well. The fall of the baht immediately raised doubts about the viability of exchange rate arrangements in the other ASEAN economies.

The Philippines was next in line, where the authorities had also been maintaining an exchange rate peg to the US dollar. The response of the Philippines government was typical. It sought briefly to defend the peso by increasing interest rates and by intervening in relevant markets; but, it was eventually forced to allow the peso to float on 11 July. In a further attempt to curtail more speculation against its currency, the authorities imposed restrictions on the sale of non-deliverable forward contracts to non-residents.

Spill-over effects spread quickly to Malaysia, where the authorities, trying to avoid the painful and costly mistakes of their Thai and Filipino neighbors, decided to allow the ringgit to depreciate gradually. This initially circumvented the option of raising interest rates, which would have hurt local businesses. Although the ringgit did not nose-dive, it embarked on a stubborn downward trend, piercing the 3 ringgit to the dollar psychological barrier on 4 September 1997. Ambivalence on the part of the Malaysian government caused further loss of confidence in the economy. It appeared that the market reacted adversely to Dr. Mahathir's call to curtail and even ban outright currency speculation. However, whatever damage was caused by Dr. Mahathir's diatribe against such activities was salvaged by concrete actions and measures undertaken by the government to deal with the situation. Malaysia resorted to self-treatment by imposing a regime of economic austerity instead of turning to the IMF for assistance. Mega-projects were deferred, measures were taken to cut current account deficit from 4% to 3% by the end of 1999, a 10% pay cut for cabinet ministers was announced, a general pay reduction in the civil service was arranged and other confidence-boosting measures and policies were also drafted during this period.

Indonesia was likewise not spared. On 12 July 1997, the rupiah fell sharply within the official intervention band. The Indonesians, after the depreciation of the peso, had adopted a wider band of 8% to 12% points, but in their case the speculative assault was relentless. The government, having failed to contain exchange market pressures, conceded letting the rupiah float on 14 August.

When the crisis affected Korea as well, things began to look increasingly worrisome. Equity prices in Korea fell dramatically, reflecting the loss of confidence in an orderly workout of the corporate debt and the growing difficulties which the financial sector was facing in rolling over external liabilities. Downward pressures on the won intensified and after a brief period of intervention by the Bank of Korea to halt the slide of the won, the authorities widened the daily fluctuation band from 4.5% to 20% on 20 November. The following day, the IMF was approached for financial support. After a few false starts which sent jitters through the markets causing the won to tumble to an all-time low of 1250 against the dollar on 2 December, the

IMF loan deal of $58 billion was signed two days later. However, this did little to placate the market, and fears of the hardship and austerity measures accompanying the IMF loan sent the won plunging to new depths of 1,745 against the dollar by 23 January 1998.

By this time the baht had fallen by a substantial 18% against the dollar, compared with the more measured fall of the other ASEAN countries of about 10%. The situation grew drastically worse over the next two months, as fears mounted over the effects of battered currencies and higher domestic interest rates on the solvency of many of the highly leveraged companies and the overly generous banks which had lent heavily to them. The situation was not helped by the fact that the authorities pussyfooted around implementing the tough measures required to restore exchange rate stability. As the crisis deepened, spill-over effects began to be felt in other Far Eastern countries as concerns about the effects on growth and export competitiveness of developments in the region intensified. Even the stronger currencies within the region such as the Singapore, New Taiwan and Hong Kong dollars came under attack.

Foreign exchange depreciation of some Asian currencies against the dollar between 1 July 1997 and 3 February.

Country	Currency	Rate of Depreciation Against the US dollar
Thailand	Baht	48% (26.07–50.00)
South Korean	Won	49% (900–1,750)
Malaysia	Ringgit	47% (2.50–4.75)
Philippines	Peso	27% (30–41)
Singapore	SingDollar	19% (1.25–1.55)
Indonesia	Rupiah	85% (2,500–17,100 on 22 Jan 1998)

Source: Bank of America

While the presence and culpability of hedge funds in precipitating the crisis in Thailand cannot be denied, their role in the other ASEAN economies has yet to be fully established. It seems that this has not been a major driving force behind the downward pressure on the other currencies. Instead, it was domestic investors, and in some cases, international commercial and investment banks that played a pivotal role in driving the domestic currencies downhill as they sought to protect themselves. By October, the combined declines of the ASEAN currencies against the dollar exceeded 30% for Indonesia and Thailand and 20% for Malaysia and the Philippines. Hence, the IMF's initial and paramount concern was to check the loss of confidence in order to prevent the currencies going into freefall.

IMF Programs in the Asian Crisis

Under the Articles of Agreement the IMF is charged with the duty of safeguarding the stability of the international monetary system. After the crisis erupted in Thailand, the contagion spread swiftly to the other economies in the region, which appeared to be susceptible to an erosion of competitiveness or were perceived by investors to have similar financial and macroeconomic problems. The international monetary system and global economy was further threatened when the contagion reached Korea, the world's eleventh largest economy, as it faced the possibility of an external debt default. The principal role that the IMF had to play in the Asian financial crisis was clear: it had to restore confidence to the ravaged economies.

The Immediate IMF General Response to the Crisis

The loss of confidence in the Korean, Indonesian and Thai (and other) economies had led to massive capital outflows from these countries which sent their respective currencies tumbling. Hence the IMF responded by helping these three countries most affected by the crisis to design programs of structural economic reforms that could win the confidence and approval of the investors. These measures were:

- the introduction of flexible exchange rates;
- a temporary tightening of monetary policy (primarily an interest rate hike) to stem pressures on the balance of payments;
- immediate action to deal with the ostensible flaws in the financial system;
- structural reforms to remove hindrances to economic growth; such as monopolies, trade barriers, etc.;
- improvements in the efficiency of financial intermediation and the future soundness of financial systems;
- ensuring external lines of credit remain open or are re-established;
- maintaining a sound and prudent fiscal policy while providing for the costs of financial sector restructuring and the uninterrupted provision of social services.

As the financial sector was a major cause of the crisis, the hallmark of the Asia programs has been the comprehensive reform of the financial systems. While bearing in mind the individual and particular needs of these countries, the program aimed to straighten out the financial sector and advocated the following measures:

- the closure of unviable financial institutions;
- the recapitalization of under-capitalized institutions;
- close supervision of weak institutions;
- increased foreign participation in domestic financial systems.

Although private sector expenditure and financing decisions led to the crisis, the situation was also not helped (in fact was exacerbated) by government involvement in the private sector. The lack of transparency in corporate and fiscal accounting and the provision of financial and economic data was an issue of grave concern, as it gave rise to speculation concerning official duplicity. Hence to address the governance issues that had contributed to the crisis the following objectives and measures were adopted:

- to break close links between business and governments;
- prudent liberalization of the capital markets;

- to increase transparency in providing economic data, especially on the position of external reserves and liabilities, and in the provision of data in the corporate and banking sectors.

This integrated three-pronged approach of the IMF to deal with the crisis-ridden countries underscores the fact that in many ways, Thailand, Indonesia and Korea face similar problems. They all have and are still suffering from an acute loss of confidence which has led to the massive depreciation of their currencies. Furthermore, these countries are plagued with weak financial systems, an excessive amount of short-term external debt borrowed by the private sector and a lack of transparency about the close links between government, banks and businesses. These things have all contributed to the crisis and have complicated efforts to deal with it.

However, these economies are also different in several important aspects. Although current account deficits have been assumed by many commentators to be a salient feature of the crisis, this is true only in regard to Thailand. While the Thai economy had been experiencing a persistent and substantial current account deficit (8% of its GDP), Korea's deficit has been narrowing, and Indonesia's was at a reasonable level of 3% of its GDP. Another important difference is that these countries called on the IMF at different stages of their troubles. When Thailand called on the doctor, the central bank was almost empty, while Korea only approached the IMF when it was on the verge of a debt default. Indonesia, on the other hand, approached the IMF for assistance at an earlier stage. But reluctance to implement the IMF program, the health of President Suharto, and contagion from Korea devastated the Indonesian economy. Hence it became necessary for the Indonesian authorities to intensify and accelerate the program.

The IMF's approach in designing support programs for these countries needed to reflect these similarities and differences. All three programs have called for a substantial rise in interest rates to stop their respective currencies from further depreciation. The programs also have advocated far-reaching structural reforms and changes to the countries' financial systems. To this end, non-viable financial institutions have had to be closed down, and remaining ones are required to come up with restructuring plans and comply with internationally-accepted best practices. Other measures, such as increasing transparency and opening the local markets, will be dealt with below.

Naturally, the fiscal programs vary from country to country. However, in each case the IMF has asked for a fiscal adjustment that will cover the carrying costs of financial sector restructuring and help restore a sustainable balance of payments.

Specific Responses of the IMF

THAILAND

Highlights of the initial program of economic reform:

- financial sector restructuring, initially focusing on the identification and closure of unviable financial institutions (including 56 out of 58 Thai finance companies), intervention in the weakest banks, and the recapitalization of the banking system;
- fiscal measures equivalent to about 3% of GDP to correct the public sector deficit to a surplus of 1% of GDP in 1997/8, to support the necessary improvement in the current account position, and to provide for the costs of financial restructuring, including an increase in the VAT tax rate from 7% to 10%;
- a new framework for monetary and exchange rate policy, featuring a managed float for the baht;
- structural initiatives to increase efficiency, deepen the role of the private sector in the Thai economy, and reinforce its outward orientation, including civil service reform, privatization, and initiatives to attract foreign capital.

Subsequent modifications as in the Letter of Intent of 25 November 1997

In light of the fact that the economy has slowed down more than anticipated and there were several adverse regional economic developments, some changes are required.
- additional actions to prevent a deterioration in the fiscal position;
- establishment of a specific timetable for implementing financial sector restructuring, including strategies for the preemptive recapitalization and strengthening of the financial system;
- acceleration of plans to protect the weaker sectors of society.

Further modifications as contained in the Letter of Intent of 24 February 1998

This was designed to send a clear signal that the utmost priority was to stabilize the exchange rate while limiting the negative social impact of the serious economic downturn. The following are some of the most significant modifications:
- accelerating financial system restructuring;
- adjusting fiscal policy targets from a targeted public sector surplus of about 1% of GDP to a deficit of about 2% GDP in response to the weakened economic activity and larger than anticipated improvement in the current account, and also to finance higher social spending;
- ensuring an adequate availability of credit to the economy to lead to economic recovery, while maintaining a tight monetary stance;
- strengthening the social safety net;
- further deepening the role of the private sector, including initiatives to attract foreign capital.

IMF Programs in the Asian Crisis

	1995	1996	1997	1998
Real GDP Growth	8.7	5.5	−0.4	−3.0
Current Account Balance	−8.0	−8.1	−2.0	3.9
External Debt	82.6	90.6	91.8	85.9

Total Financing Committed: $57 billion, of which:
    The Fund $21 billion
    World Bank $10 billion
    Asian Development Bank $4 billion
    Group of Industrial Countries $22 billion

INDONESIA

When the crisis first began, Indonesia was not thought to be as vulnerable as Thailand. However, as events unfolded, structural weaknesses in the Indonesian economy became disturbingly evident. Of particular concern was the large amount of foreign debt owed by the private corporate sector. On 5 November, the IMF's Executive Board approved financial support of up to $10 billion over the next three years.

The initial program of economic reform included:

- financial sector restructuring, including closing unviable institutions, merging state banks and establishing a timetable for dealing with remaining weak institutions and improving the institutional, legal and regulatory framework of the financial system;
- structural reforms to enhance economic efficiency and transparency, including the liberalization of foreign trade and investment, dismantling domestic monopolies, and expanding privatization programs;
- stabilizing the rupiah by adopting a tight monetary policy of high interest rates and a flexible exchange rate regime;
- fiscal measures equivalent to about 1% of GDP in 1997/8 and 2% in 1998/9, to yield a public sector surplus of 1% of GDP in both periods, to facilitate external adjustment and provide

resources to pay for financial restructuring. The fiscal measures include cutting back from major state enterprise infrastructure projects; removing government subsidies; eliminating VAT exemptions, and adjusting administered prices, including the prices of petroleum products and electricity.

Despite these measures, the IMF and the Indonesian authorities failed to stem the continued loss of confidence in the economy and the rupiah experienced acute depreciation. In response, the Indonesian authorities announced a reinforcement and acceleration of the program in the 'Memorandum of Economic and Financial Policies' issued on 15 January 1998. The main features are:

- adjustment to the 1998/9 budget that would result in a public sector deficit of about 1% of GDP, in order to absorb part of the impact on the budget of the economic slowdown;
- the cancellation of 12 infrastructure projects and the revoking or discontinuation of privileges for the IPTN's airline projects and the National Car project;
- more far-reaching bank and corporate sector restructuring; which included the announcement of a framework for creditors and debtors to work on the external debt problems of Indonesian corporations on a voluntary, case-by-case basis;
- the establishment of the Indonesian Bank Restructuring Agency (IBRA); and a government guarantee on bank deposits and credits;
- limiting the monopoly of the national marketing board (BULOG) to rice, deregulating domestic trade in agricultural produce, and eliminating restrictive market arrangements;
- measures to alleviate the suffering caused by the drought, and to ensure that adequate food supplies are available at reasonable prices.

Still the rupiah refused to stabilize and continued to fall sharply; inflation picked up drastically and the general economic conditions deteriorated. This led the government to issue a 'Supplementary

Memorandum of Economic and Financial Policies' on 10 April 1998 to lend weight to its earlier policies. The added measures included:

- a stronger monetary policy to stop the rupiah from sliding further;
- accelerated bank restructuring, with IBRA to continue with its closing or takeover of unviable or weak financial institutions. It was also empowered to issue bonds to finance the restoration of financial viability to qualified institutions; existing restrictions on foreign ownership of banks were removed; and a new bankruptcy law was passed;
- a comprehensive agenda of structural reforms to increase competition and efficiency in the economy, reinforcing the commitments made in January and including the privatization of a further six major state enterprises and the identification of seven new enterprises for privatization in 1998/9;
- accelerated arrangement to develop a framework with foreign creditors to restore trade financing and to resolve the issue of corporate debt and interbank credit;
- strengthening the social safety net through support for small and medium sized enterprises and through public work programs;
- enhancing the implementation and creditability of the program through daily monitoring by the Indonesian Executive Committee of the Resilience Council, in close cooperation with the IMF, the World Bank, and the ADB; substantive actions prior to approval of the program by the IMF Executive Board, and frequent program reviews by the IMF Executive board.

	1995	1996	1997	1998
Real GDP Growth	8.2	8.0	4.6	−5.0
Current Account Balance	−3.2	−3.3	−1.2	2.7
External Debt	106.5	113.3	119.6	112.8

KOREA

The Korean economy was the envy of the world. It grew consistently over the past few decades to become the world's 11th largest economy. However, the financial system had been weakened by government influence in the economy and the close links between banks and conglomerates. The enormous short-term external debt threatened to bring the entire economy to a virtual standstill. On 4 December 1997 the IMF's Executive Board approved financing of $21 billion over the next three years.

The initial program of economic reform:

- comprehensive financial sector restructuring that introduced a clear and firm exit policy for financial institutions, strong market and supervisory discipline, and independence for the central bank. The operations of nine insolvent merchant banks were suspended; two large distressed commercial banks received capital injections from the government, and all commercial banks with inadequate capital were required to submit plans for recapitalization;
- fiscal measures equivalent to about 2% of GDP to make room for the costs of financial sector restructuring in the budget, while maintaining a prudent fiscal stance. Fiscal measures include the widening of the tax base: corporate, income and VAT;
- efforts to dismantle the non-transparent and inefficient ties between government, banks, and businesses. Accounting, auditing and disclosure standards are to be made more stringent; corporate financial statements are to be prepared on a consolidated basis and certified by external auditors; and the system of cross guarantees within conglomerates is to be changed;
- trade liberalization measures: setting a timetable in line with WTO commitments to eliminate trade-related subsidies, a restrictive import licensing and import diversification program, and streamlining and improving transparency of import certification procedures;

- capital account liberalization measures to open up the Korean money, equity and bond market to capital inflows and to liberalize foreign direct investment;
- labor market reform to facilitate redeployment of labor; and
- the publication and dissemination of key economic and financial data.

The program was subsequently intensified as the financial crisis in Korea worsened and concerns about whether international banks would roll over the short-term external debt exerted tremendous pressures on the international reserves and the won. On 24 December in a Letter of Intent the Korean authorities made revision to the prior measures:

- further monetary tightening and the abolition of the daily exchange rate band;
- speeding up the liberalization of capital and money markets, including the lifting of all capital account restrictions on foreign investors' access to the Korean bond market by 3 December 1997;
- accelerating the implementation of the comprehensive restructuring plan for the financial sector, including establishing a high-level team to negotiate with foreign creditors and reduce the recourse of Korean banks to the central bank;
- speeding up trade liberalization measures, including making the liberalization of financial services as agreed with OECD binding under the WTO.

After meeting with some partial success, the macroeconomic framework was revised and the policies that the government intended to pursue for 1998 were set out in a Letter of Intent on 7 February 1998. The measures include:

- targeting a fiscal deficit of around 1% of GDP for 1998 to accommodate the impact of weaker economic activity on the budget and to allow for higher expenditure on the social safety net;

- moving forward to implement a broader strategy of financial sector restructuring, having contained the immediate dangers of disruptions to the financial system;
- increasing the range and amounts of financial instruments available to foreign investors, increasing the access of Korean companies to foreign capital markets, and liberalizing the corporate financing market;
- introducing a number of measures to improve corporate transparency, including strengthening the oversight functions of corporate boards of directors, increasing accountability to shareholders, and introducing outside directors and external audit committees.

Additional Measures Taken by the IMF

As reinforcement to the first line of response taken by the IMF — assisting in the design of the programs and providing required financial resources for its implementation, further measures have been adopted:

- the Executive Board made use of the accelerated procedures to meet the needs of the affected member countries. Hence they are entitled to greater access to the Fund's credit facilities;
- the Supplemental Reserve Facility was created, for the special circumstances of dire balance of payments imbalances resulting from a large short-term financing need;
- the coordination of the IMF with other international financial institutions, notably the World Bank and the Asian Development Bank and with bilateral donors. This is a clear signal of international cooperation and support to deal with the Asian crisis;
- a strengthened level of dialogue between the IMF and the countries affected, including consultations with the labor groups and extensive contacts with the press and public;
- IMF programs have been followed by coordinated efforts between international creditor banks and debtors in the affected countries

to resolve the severe private sector financing problems. The IMF has provided support to this process;
- IMF member countries have attained new levels of transparency through the release of Letters of Intent describing their programs of economic reform. The Letters of Intent from Indonesia, Korea and Thailand are available on the IMF website (http://www.imf.org);
- the appointment of former IMF Deputy Managing Director Prabhakar Narvekar as Special Advisor to the president of Indonesia; the establishment of resident representative posts in Korea and Thailand; and other activities conducted through the new IMF's Asia and Pacific Regional Office;
- the IMF is answering the requests it has received from its members, directly and via multilateral forums such as the Group of Seven and the Group of Twenty-Four nations, to investigate aspects related to the financial crisis, including the role of hedge funds, the strengthening of financial sector soundness, and implications for the global financial architecture.

The crisis in Asia has highlighted the volatility of the international finance system and the IMF has begun to draw lessons from it on how to strengthen the architecture of the system to lessen the frequency and severity of future disturbances. These are:

- more effective surveillance over a nation's economic policies and practices, facilitated by fuller disclosure of all relevant economic and financial data. The IMF has established, and will further improve, data standards to guide members in releasing reliable and timely data to the public;
- financial sector reform, including more prudential regulation and supervision. Working with the Basle Committee on Banking Supervision and the World Bank, the Fund has helped develop and disseminate a set of 'best practices' in the banking area;
- the fostering of orderly and properly-sequenced capital account liberalization (supported by a sound financial sector and appropriate

macroeconomics and exchange rate policies) in order to maximize the benefits from and minimize the risk of free capital movements;
- promoting regional surveillance;
- encouraging and supporting the worldwide effort to fight against corruption and promote good governance;
- establishing more effective structures for orderly debt workouts, including better bankruptcy laws at national level and, at international level, better ways of associating private sector creditors and investors with official efforts to help resolve sovereign and private debt problems.

All of the above measures support the long-term objective of the IMF's response to the Asian financial crisis, which is to enable the affected Asian economies to regain economic vigor in order to resume rapid development, and to help fortify the international monetary system against such crises in the future.

Criticisms of the IMF

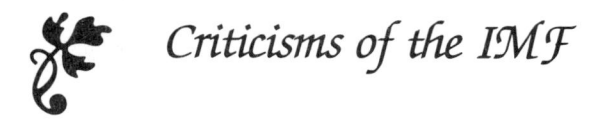

Partly the inevitable result of its high profile and (enviable?) sway over world economics, and partly due to some egregious misjudgements in the current crisis, a number of criticims have been leveled at the IMF, in both academia and the popular media. A number of these, and some responses by the IMF, are outlined in this chapter.

It Is Far Too Harsh

The IMF has been widely criticized for demanding excessively tight fiscal and monetary policies in its bail out packages for Indonesia, South Korea and Thailand. The stock-in-trade IMF prescription, it is argued, is not appropriate for East Asian economies; and worse, these measures may actually exacerbate the crisis by driving the countries into recession. Blinded by the success of these measures in an earlier bail out in Mexico, it may be imprudent for the IMF to impose the same restrictive policies in Asia. While such belt tightening may have been appropriate in Mexico, given that the current account deficit was the consequence of extravagant consumption, the cause of the deficits in these Asian economies were the result of high investment. Besides, the weaknesses in these Asian economies, although substantial, were according to Harvard economist Jeffery Sachs 'far from fatal'. In other words, these economies' deeper strengths — such as high rates of savings, budget surpluses, a flexible and trained workforce, and low taxation — remain intact and place them in a position for recovery. Thus, the Fund's bitter pill of getting governments to cut back on expenditure and to tighten domestic bank credit by increasing interest and the forced closing of weak banks only served to erode investor confidence. This resulted in a 'stampede mentality' which led to further capital flight and economic contraction. The claim was that high interest rates and fiscal austerity will incur widespread bankruptcies, without any definite assurance that the currencies will stop sliding.

Response

Are these programs therefore unnecessarily tough? When these countries approached the IMF, they were in dire financial straits. The international reserves of Thailand and Korea were perilously low, and the Indonesian rupiah has suffered from excessive depreciation. Hence, the utmost priority was to restore confidence and stabilize their respective currencies. In order to achieve this, it is vital that these countries make it relatively attractive to hold domestic currencies — which requires increasing interest rates temporarily. This is absolutely necessary despite the fact that higher domestic interest rates may cause complications and bankruptcies in the weaker banks and corporations. Without this interest rate increase, there is a real risk that these currencies may go into free fall, increasing the debt burden in domestic currency and severely hurting borrowers who must pay off their foreign currency dominated liabilities. Once confidence is restored, interest rates can return to more normal levels.

Besides, from the viewpoint of the international system, the devaluations in Asian currencies will lead to large trade surpluses in those countries and damage the competitive positions of other countries. This may spark another round of devaluation elsewhere, hence spreading the crisis. Finally, although results have been mixed, the recent experiences of Latin America, the Czech Republic and Hong Kong imply that raising interest rates to fend off attacks on currency can achieve some measure of success.

On the question of the appropriate level of fiscal tightening, the balance is a particularly fine one. At the onset of the crisis, countries needed to adjust their fiscal positions, both to make room in their budgets for the future costs of financial restructuring, and to reduce the current account deficit. Moreover, the fiscal costs involved in the restructuring program were divided over an extended period rather than concentrated at the beginning of the crisis. For instance, if the costs of the financial reforms is expected to amount to 15% of the GDP, then the corresponding fiscal adjustment for a single period would be 1.5% of the GDP.

Following this approach, the amount of fiscal adjustment in Indonesia was 1% of the GDP, in Korea it was about 1.5% and in Thailand the initial adjustment was 3% of the GDP — reflecting its large current account deficit. However, as the economic conditions in these three countries have deteriorated, the IMF has agreed to the widening of the deficit.

Thus in macroeconomic terms, the answer to the critics is that monetary policy has to be kept tight to restore confidence in the currency, and that fiscal policy must tighten correspondingly at the start of each program, with greater flexibility permitted to address the worsening situation. As market confidence and the currencies continue to strengthen, interest rates could be allowed to come down.

The IMF Programs Have Made the Situation Worse

According to Dr. Sachs, while the IMF's harsh macroeocnomic regime could be theoretically sound, the incontrovertible fact is that it simply has not worked. The criticism was made that the Fund is too mechanical in its approach: it just blundered in and made matters worse.

IMF and the Asian Financial Crisis

Other points that have been made include:

The IMF should concentrate on the 'things that caused the crisis, not on things that make it more difficult to deal with', according to the World Bank's chief economist, Joseph Stiglitz.

"The IMF has got it comprehensively wrong in its approach to Asia and instead of being part of the solution, it is now part of the problem," says Ajay Kapur, Asia Equity Strategist at UBS securities.

Response

While the IMF has admitted that it initially erred in requiring the Indonesian government to implement tough budget tightening measures, it has shown itself to be flexible and modest enough to make the necessary adjustments. For example, in January 1998, Thai Prime Minister Chuan Leekpai requested the IMF to relax the terms of its $17 billion package, as it was impossible for the Thais to produce a budget surplus. Recognizing that its projection was based on 'optimistic assumptions' and following the Fund's second review in February 1998, the IMF made the appropriate adjustments.

While the Fund failed to arrest the currency decline, it does not follow that it was therefore culpable for it. The baht's sharp decline had more to do with the erratic nature of investor confidence and the spreading contagion than the IMF's insistence for austerity and credit contraction. Malaysia, which has not received financial assistance or been placed under any of the Fund's strict programs, also witnessed its currency taking a beating. Similarly the extreme peaks and troughs experienced by the Indonesian rupiah from 2,400 against the US dollar to 17,100 at one point was the result of domestic political uncertainties rather than the ineffectual IMF programs. In fact, the markets were responding adversely to the arbitrary delays by the Suharto regime in implementing the IMF program and to the appointment of technophile

Dr. B.J. Habibie, Suharto's long-time friend, as his Vice-President. Habibie, who has major financial stakes in many business activities in Indonesia, was seen as one of the icons of crony capitalism and perverse patrimonialist business subculture for which the suddenly self-righteous market had little tolerance.

Moral Hazard

The IMF has also been accused of creating moral hazard by coming to the assistance of countries in crisis. The more the IMF bails out countries, the more likely countries are to slip into crises in the future because risky behavior on the part of their government may be encouraged and investors might come to expect that if anything goes wrong, the IMF will come to the rescue. Governments will not be discouraged from maintaining flawed policies as long as lenders keep the capital flowing. Lenders, for their part, behaved imprudently with the knowledge that government money would be used in case of financial troubles. That knowledge does not, however, mean that investors are indifferent toward the possibility of a crisis; but it can lead to the mispricing of risk and to a distortion in the investment calculations of lenders. In short, moral hazard leads to indiscriminate lending. In this regard, the prior Mexican bail out initiated by the IMF could be held partly responsible for the present crisis in Asia. Furthermore, the financial aid from the IMF cuts investors' losses rather than allowing them to bear the full responsibility for their decisions. The $57 billion committed to Korea didn't help anybody but the banks, noted Jeffery Sachs. Unfortunately for the ordinary Asian citizens who had nothing to do with creating the crisis, they will be forced to pay for the added debt burden imposed by the IMF loans.

Response

The criticism that the IMF's assistance to Korea, Indonesia and Thailand bails out specific groups such as commercial banks and private investors at the expense of other less favored groups and taxpayers is simply inaccurate. The IMF reiterates the fact that its assistance has been provided in support of programs that are designed to deal with the causes and consequences of economy-wide structural imbalances and the potential threats these imbalances pose to the international monetary system. And under the condition for these programs, commercial banks and private investors are being protected from financial losses. There are no provisions in the IMF-supported programs for public sector guarantees, subsidies or support for non-financial institutions that are facing financial difficulties and may be forced into bankruptcy. And when financial sectors are restructured, shareholders and, as far as possible, creditors of insolvent institutions should bear the losses they would have sustained in the context of liquidation under bankruptcy procedures.

Regarding the theory that, given the IMF 'safety-net', investors would not appraise risks accurately and hence be all too willing to lend to countries with dubious economies, this is perhaps rather far-fetched. Evidence shows that many countries avoid approaching the Fund, even when in trouble, because of the tough measures which accompany the loans. And neither have the individual policy-makers whose countries end in economic turmoil survived politically. In this sense, there is a lot of pressure for the authorities to do the right thing. The argument that if investors are bailed out inappropriately, they will be less careful in the future does not seem to be consistent with reality. Most investors in the Asian crisis countries have suffered very heavy losses. This is true of equity investors and of those who have lent to corporations and banks. With the stock markets and exchange rates plunging, foreign equity investors had by the end of 1997 lost nearly three-quarters of the value of their equity holdings in some Asian markets. Many firms and financial institutions will go bankrupt and their foreign and domestic lenders will share in the losses.

While the existence of moral hazard is not denied, its purported effects are obviously limited. Investors have been hit hard and will not simply conclude from the crisis that they need not worry about the risks of their lending because the IMF will come to their rescue in the future.

However, this still begs the question: What caused the unwise lending that underlies the Asian crisis, if it were not the phenomenon of moral hazard? The answer is probably irrational exuberance.

Financial crises are dependent on swings in investors' confidence, on irrational exuberance and irrational depression — irrational, that is, not in that they lack some foundation in fact, but in representing an *excessive* reaction. Hence the role for the Fund in this respect is clear: to provide the information and incentives that will encourage rational investor behavior. The role of IMF lending should be viewed in this light rather than as simplistic bail outs. When the IMF lends in a crisis, it helps moderate the recession that the country inevitably faces. This means that the residents of that country, its corporations and some of the that country's creditors, fare better than they otherwise would have done. That is not a bail out in any literal sense but represents rational lending under conditions when markets appear to have overreacted. Moreover, when the IMF provides financial assistance, it aims to be repaid, and is not simply giving money away.

Unnecessary and Excessive Interference

In the Mexican crisis, Mexico and other Latin American countries could not meet the interest and principal payments on their large external liabilities. A default of this magnitude would have decimated the capital of leading banks in the United States, Europe and Japan, so the US government provided a temporary bridge loan that allowed Mexico to satisfy its most immediate payments. Negotiations were then carried out between the Mexican government and the lending banks that had agreed to restructure the debts, lengthen the maturities and lend additional money. Over time, the process was successful.

The Latin American economies eventually picked up, and the countries were able to service their rescheduled debts. In the Asian case, instead of relying on private banks and serving its role as a monitor of performance, the IMF intervened and took the lead in providing credit. Might it have been more effective for the IMF to provide a bridging loan and then organize the banks involved into a negotiating group, instead of prescribing a fundamental overhaul of the afflicted economies? The IMF's role in Thailand and Indonesia may be said to have gone beyond its mandate, by imposing programs requiring governments to reform their financial institutions and to make substantial changes in their economic frameworks and political practices. The legitimate political institutions of the country should determine the nation's economic structure and the nature of its institutions. One could argue that a nation's desperate need for short-term financial help does not give the IMF the right to apply its technical judgments in place of the nation's own political agenda. It should not use the opportunity to impose other economic changes that are not necessary to deal with the balance of payments problem and are the proper responsibility of the country's own political system.

Response

Admittedly the IMF programs entail far-reaching reforms that may directly or indirectly influence and alter economic structure and institutions. This broadening of the scope of IMF policy concerns has met with mixed reactions. While some have applauded the Fund for tackling the structural problems and governance issues that stand in the way of growth, others have also condemned the IMF for excessive intrusion into what are regarded as essentially the domestic affairs of sovereign states. Nonetheless, financial sector restructuring lies at the heart of the programs in Indonesia, Korea and Thailand. This is simply because of weak financial institutions, inadequate bank regulation and supervision, and the complicated and non-transparent relations among governments, banks and corporations that were a major cause of the crisis.

It would not serve any lasting purpose for the IMF to lend to these countries unless these problems were addressed. Nor would it be in those countries' interests to leave the structural and governance issues unaddressed. It has been proven that markets remain skeptical where reforms have been incomplete or uncommitted and as a result confidence has failed to be restored. There is neither point nor excuse for the international community to provide financial assistance to a country unless that country adopts measures to prevent such crises in the future. That is the fundamental reason behind the inclusion of structural changes in Fund-supported programs.

The alternative approach of leaving countries and their creditors to sort out the country's inability to service its debts is not simple. Experience from the inter-war period and the 1980s has shown that workouts tend to be protracted and that countries have been denied market access for a long duration at an inimical cost to growth. Further, the IMF had to act swiftly in order to help economies avoid virtually grinding to a halt, in which case the potential of contagion would become a real risk.

Painful Social Costs

Insufficient attention has been paid to the social impact of the crisis and its concomitant remedies. There is a real danger that the fiscal austerity imposed by the IMF entails a dramatic cut in social spending and threatens to roll back the significant social advances made in poverty reduction over the recent decades in these economies, particularly Thailand and Indonesia. In Indonesia, Oxfam estimates that the number of people living below the poverty line could well reach

1977 figures — that is, approximately 40% of its vast population. Human suffering is on the increase, with unemployment reaching unprecedented levels. A sharp rise in the price of food items and other necessities seems imminent, especially with the breakdown of the distribution of basic goods and services. Reductions in public spending could thus act as a driving force for poverty, reducing basic services to the poor at precisely the time when they need them most urgently. The IMF should act to protect social spending.

Response

The IMF's mandate is to promote international monetary cooperation, balanced growth of international trade and a stable system of exchange rates; fulfilling this mandate is the IMF's primary contribution to sustainable economic and human development. To this end, IMF-supported programs have increasingly provided for an enlargement in the level and quality of public expenditure in social services, including primary education and health, as well as for improved access to these services. The IMF's technical assistance in the context of surveillance and IMF-supported programs has helped strengthen policy design and institutional capacity for implementing economic and social policies. In the fiscal area, technical assistance has focused on the design of sustainable social safety nets, improved management of public expenditure (including social programs) and efficiency and greater equity of tax policy and administration.

The IMF is also working closely with the World Bank and other UN agencies in the design, implementation, and monitoring of social policies. The IMF is continuously seeking to improve policy advice and program design, based on past experience. In the social area, there is a particular need to help governments to improve the integration of social aspects in their wider programs, as well as the composition of their expenditure and revenues. The Fund has also recognized the need to encourage them to better address structural weaknesses in the rural areas, where most of the poor live.

A New Chapter: Lessons for the International Financial System

Present developments in South-east Asia have shown that there are very serious risks associated with financial globalization. Developing countries are more susceptible to shifts in market sentiment regarding the economic situation. Changes in market perception can trigger massive movements of capital that can in turn precipitate banking sector crises and have adverse spill-over effects on other countries. But this should not obscure the benefits that can be reaped from global financial markets. They give countries new opportunities to quicken the pace of investment, job creation and growth. They give investors a wider range of investment opportunities and higher returns from savings. More importantly, they promote a more efficient allocation of resources worldwide and hence stronger world growth. However, some countries that are not adequately developed and well equipped to take advantage of this expansion of trade and finance risk becoming marginalized.

The balance of benefits and risks facing countries in the global economy depends largely on how swiftly countries adapt to the new global economic environment and how quickly and appropriately they react to changes in this environment and in their own domestic economies. Of course, there are many challenges that exceed the capacity of individual countries acting alone, and partnership both at regional and international levels in this increasingly interdependent world is therefore absolutely crucial. Here the IMF plays an equally important role to help all member countries deal with these changes in the global economy.

The focus now is on the architecture of the international system, specifically crisis-prevention through the arrangements for monitoring and regulating flows of international capital, and crisis-response to improve the system's reaction when a crisis occurs.

The IMF's Envisaged Role in Global Cooperation

There is a need to increase the flow of timely, accurate and comprehensive data to the public. Through the Special Data Dissemination Standard, the IMF is encouraging countries to move toward greater transparency and fuller disclosure; and it will be necessary to strengthen the standard, for instance by providing data on forward transactions by central banks. Better data provision should lead not only to better-informed investor decisions, but also to better policies by governments. Some of the off-balance-sheet activities of central banks that were instrumental in the recent crisis could not have continued for as long as they did if the public had had full knowledge of the situation. It is also clear from the present crisis that there is a real need for better and more timely data on short-term debt exposures, not only of banks, but also of corporations. The Bank of International Settlements, which is committed to improving the short-term debt situation, is already providing excellent information in this area.

Ways need to be found to enhance the effectiveness of Fund surveillance — by ensuring among other things that all the relevant data is being supplied to the Fund; that countries' exchange rate regimes are consistent with other policies; and that capital inflows are sustainable. The question of whether the Fund should provide more public information and if necessary issue public warning of impending trouble is also on the agenda. Many have argued that the efficient functioning of the international system requires greater transparency at the IMF itself. This is happening and should continue.

Since crises are often provoked by problems in the financial sector or intensified by them, much more needs to be done to strengthen domestic financial systems. The IMF has been working in this area by helping to develop and disseminate a set of best practices in banking, so that standards and practices that have worked well in some countries can be adapted and applied in others. These standards are codified in the Basle Committee on Banking Supervision's 25 core principles, introduced in 1997. However, mechanisms to monitor the implementation of the standards also need to be developed to ensure that countries continue to conform to them.

There is an urgent need to improve the way capital markets operate in both advanced and emerging market countries. One possibility would be to encourage countries to adopt international standards in areas needed for the smooth operation of financial markets, such as bankruptcy codes, securities trading and corporate governance, including accounting. Market participants would then have a clearer basis for making their lending decisions. Once again the international system would need to find a way of monitoring the implementation of these standards, and this is a formidable task. Observance of these standards would be encouraged if the risk-weighting on international loans applied by bank regulators in the lending countries reflected compliance of the borrowing countries with the standards.

One thing is for certain: the global economy is in a constant state of flux and international financial shocks are likely to happen from time to time in the future. How frequent and severe these shocks occur will be the main measure of success or failure for the IMF.

Appendix: Key Articles of Agreement of the IMF

ARTICLE I: Purposes

The purposes of the International Monetary Fund are:

(i) To promote international monetary cooperation through a permanent institution which provides the machinery for consultation and collaboration on international monetary problems.
(ii) To facilitate the expansion and balanced growth of international trade, and to contribute thereby to the promotion and maintenance of high levels of employment and real income and to the development of the productive resources of all members as primary objectives of economic policy.
(iii) To promote exchange stability, to maintain orderly exchange arrangements among members, and to avoid competitive exchange depreciation.
(iv) To assist in the establishment of a multilateral system of payments in respect of current transactions between members and in the elimination of foreign exchange restrictions which hamper the growth of world trade.
(v) To give confidence to members by making the general resources of the Fund temporarily available to them under adequate

Appendix

safeguards, thus providing them with opportunity to correct maladjustments in their balance of payments without resorting to measures destructive of national or international prosperity.

(vi) In accordance with the above, to shorten the duration and lessen the degree of disequilibrium in the international balances of payments of members.

The Fund shall be guided in all its policies and decisions by the purposes set forth in this Article.

ARTICLE IV: Obligations Regarding Exchange Arrangements

Section 1. General obligations of members

Recognizing that the essential purpose of the international monetary system is to provide a framework that facilitates the exchange of goods, services, and capital among countries, and that sustains sound economic growth, and that a principal objective is the continuing development of the orderly underlying conditions that are necessary for financial and economic stability, each member undertakes to collaborate with the Fund and other members to assure orderly exchange arrangements and to promote a stable system of exchange rates. In particular, each member shall:

(i) endeavor to direct its economic and financial policies toward the objective of fostering orderly economic growth with reasonable price stability, with due regard to its circumstances;

(ii) seek to promote stability by fostering orderly underlying economic and financial conditions and a monetary system that does not tend to produce erratic disruptions;

(iii) avoid manipulating exchange rates or the international monetary system in order to prevent effective balance of payments adjustment or to gain an unfair competitive advantage over other members; and

(iv) follow exchange policies compatible with the undertakings under this Section.

Section 2. General exchange arrangements

(a) Each member shall notify the Fund, within thirty days after the date of the second amendment of this Agreement, of the exchange arrangements it intends to apply in fulfillment of its obligations under Section 1 of this Article, and shall notify the Fund promptly of any changes in its exchange arrangements.

Appendix

(b) Under an international monetary system of the kind prevailing on January 1, 1976, exchange arrangements may include (i) the maintenance by a member of a value for its currency in terms of the special drawing right or another denominator, other than gold, selected by the member, or (ii) cooperative arrangements by which members maintain the value of their currencies in relation to the value of the currency or currencies of other members, or (iii) other exchange arrangements of a member's choice.

(c) To accord with the development of the international monetary system, the Fund, by an eighty-five percent majority of the total voting power, may make provision for general exchange arrangements without limiting the right of members to have exchange arrangements of their choice consistent with the purposes of the Fund and the obligations under Section 1 of this Article.

Section 3. Surveillance over exchange arrangements

(a) The Fund shall oversee the international monetary system in order to ensure its effective operation, and shall oversee the compliance of each member with its obligations under Section 1 of this Article.

(b) In order to fulfill its functions under (a) above, the Fund shall exercise firm surveillance over the exchange rate policies of members, and shall adopt specific principles for the guidance of all members with respect to those policies. Each member shall provide the Fund with the information necessary for such surveillance, and, when requested by the Fund, shall consult with it on the member's exchange rate policies. The principles adopted by the Fund shall be consistent with cooperative arrangements by which members maintain the value of their currencies in relation to the value of the currency or currencies of other members, as well as with other exchange arrangements of a member's choice consistent with the purposes of the Fund and Section 1 of this Article. These principles shall respect the domestic social and political policies of members, and in applying these principles the Fund shall pay due regard to the circumstances of members.

Section 4. Par values

The Fund may determine, by an eighty-five percent majority of the total voting power, that international economic conditions permit the introduction of a widespread system of exchange arrangements based on stable but adjustable par values. The Fund shall make the determination on the basis of the underlying stability of the world economy, and for this purpose shall take into account price movements and rates of expansion in the economies of members. The determination shall be made in light of the evolution of the international monetary system, with particular reference to sources of liquidity, and, in order to ensure the effective operation of a system of par values, to arrangements under which both members in surplus and members in deficit in their balances of payments take prompt, effective, and symmetrical action to achieve adjustment, as well as to arrangements for intervention and the treatment of imbalances. Upon making such determination, the Fund shall notify members that the provisions of Schedule C apply.

Section 5. Separate currencies within a member's territories

(a) Action by a member with respect to its currency under this Article shall be deemed to apply to the separate currencies of all territories in respect of which the member has accepted this Agreement under Article XXXI, Section 2(g) unless the member declares that its action relates either to the metropolitan currency alone, or only to one or more specified separate currencies, or to the metropolitan currency and one or more specified separate currencies.

(b) Action by the Fund under this Article shall be deemed to relate to all currencies of a member referred to in (a) above unless the Fund declares otherwise.

Appendix

ARTICLE VIII: General Obligations of Members

Section 1. Introduction

In addition to the obligations assumed under other articles of this Agreement, each member undertakes the obligations set out in this Article.

Section 2. Avoidance of restrictions on current payments

(a) Subject to the provisions of Article VII, Section 3(b) and Article XIV, Section 2, no member shall, without the approval of the Fund, impose restrictions on the making of payments and transfers for current international transactions.

(b) Exchange contracts which involve the currency of any member and which are contrary to the exchange control regulations of that member maintained or imposed consistently with this Agreement shall be unenforceable in the territories of any member. In addition, members may, by mutual accord, cooperate in measures for the purpose of making the exchange control regulations of either member more effective, provided that such measures and regulations are consistent with this Agreement.

Section 3. Avoidance of discriminatory currency practices

No member shall engage in, or permit any of its fiscal agencies referred to in Article V, Section 1 to engage in, any discriminatory currency arrangements or multiple currency practices, whether within or outside margins under Article IV or prescribed by or under Schedule C, except as authorized under this Agreement or approved by the Fund. If such arrangements and practices are engaged in at the date when this Agreement enters into force, the member concerned shall consult with the Fund as to their progressive removal unless they are maintained or imposed under Article XIV, Section 2, in which case the provisions of Section 3 of that Article shall apply.

Section 4. Convertibility of foreign-held balances

(a) Each member shall buy balances of its currency held by another member if the latter, in requesting the purchase, represents:

  (i) that the balances to be bought have been recently acquired as a result of current transactions; or
  (ii) that their conversion is needed for making payments for current transactions.

The buying member shall have the option to pay either in special drawing rights, subject to Article XIX, Section 4, or in the currency of the member making the request.

(b) The obligation in (a) above shall not apply when:

  (i) the convertibility of the balances has been restricted consistently with Section 2 of this Article or Article VI, Section 3;
  (ii) the balances have accumulated as a result of transactions effected before the removal by a member of restrictions maintained or imposed under Article XIV, Section 2;
  (iii) the balances have been acquired contrary to the exchange regulations of the member which is asked to buy them;
  (iv) the currency of the member requesting the purchase has been declared scarce under Article VII, Section 3(a); or
  (v) the member requested to make the purchase is for any reason not entitled to buy currencies of other members from the Fund for its own currency.

Section 5. Furnishing of information

(a) The Fund may require members to furnish it with such information as it deems necessary for its activities, including, as the minimum necessary for the effective discharge of the Fund's duties, national data on the following matters:

Appendix

(i) official holdings at home and abroad of (1) gold, (2) foreign exchange;
(ii) holdings at home and abroad by banking and financial agencies, other than official agencies, of (1) gold, (2) foreign exchange;
(iii) production of gold;
(iv) gold exports and imports according to countries of destination and origin;
(v) total exports and imports of merchandise, in terms of local currency values, according to countries of destination and origin;
(vi) international balance of payments, including (1) trade in goods and services, (2) gold transactions, (3) known capital transactions, and (4) other items;
(vii) international investment position, i.e., investments within the territories of the member owned abroad and investments abroad owned by persons in its territories so far as it is possible to furnish this information;
(viii) national income;
(ix) price indices, i.e., indices of commodity prices in wholesale and retail markets and of export and import prices;
(x) buying and selling rates for foreign currencies;
(xi) exchange controls, i.e., a comprehensive statement of exchange controls in effect at the time of assuming membership in the Fund and details of subsequent changes as they occur; and
(xii) where official clearing arrangements exist, details of amounts awaiting clearance in respect of commercial and financial transactions, and of the length of time during which such arrears have been outstanding.

(b) In requesting information the Fund shall take into consideration the varying ability of members to furnish the data requested. Members shall be under no obligation to furnish information in such detail that the affairs of individuals or corporations are disclosed. Members undertake, however, to furnish the desired information in as detailed and accurate a manner as is practicable and, so far as possible, to avoid mere estimates.

(c) The Fund may arrange to obtain further information by agreement with members. It shall act as a centre for the collection and exchange of information on monetary and financial problems, thus facilitating the preparation of studies designed to assist members in developing policies which further the purposes of the Fund.

Section 6. Consultation between members regarding existing international agreements

Where under this Agreement a member is authorized in the special or temporary circumstances specified in the Agreement to maintain or establish restrictions on exchange transactions, and there are other engagements between members entered into prior to this Agreement which conflict with the application of such restrictions, the parties to such engagements shall consult with one another with a view to making such mutually acceptable adjustments as may be necessary. The provisions of this Article shall be without prejudice to the operation of Article VII, Section 5.

Section 7. Obligation to collaborate regarding policies on reserve assets

Each member undertakes to collaborate with the Fund and with other members in order to ensure that the policies of the member with respect to reserve assets shall be consistent with the objectives of promoting better international surveillance of international liquidity and making the special drawing right the principal reserve asset in the international monetary system.